IL 11774×2

SOUNDINGS

KU-396-994

Soundings

*A selection of poems for
speaking aloud*

Edited for the Poetry Society
by
KIT WRIGHT

HEINEMANN
LONDON

Heinemann Educational Books Ltd
LONDON EDINBURGH MELBOURNE AUCKLAND TORONTO
HONG KONG SINGAPORE KUALA LUMPUR
IBADAN NAIROBI LUSAKA
JOHANNESBURG NEW DELHI

ISBN 0 435 14910 5 (cased)
0 435 14911 3 (paper)

Published by
Heinemann Educational Books Ltd
48 Charles Street, London W1X 8AH
Printed and bound in Great Britain by
Morrison & Gibb Ltd, London and Edinburgh

Contents

Introduction

If poetry is the kind of writing furthest removed from the purveying of factual information (and perhaps that's as reliable a definition as any), it is also true that poetry, unlike a column of statistics, a medical case history or a critical review, demands to be heard. All poetry is for speaking, if not aloud, then to oneself as one reads it on the page. For that reason the melodies and rhythms of the best poems are inseparable from the images they create, the view of the world they offer, the realities they are. It is a rhetorical art.

That adjective has become a favourite weapon in the critics' pejorative arsenal, but just as Chaucer was familiar with the medieval rule-books of rhetoric and employed their devices, so poets of every period have learned and adapted, consciously or unconsciously, ancient rhetorical techniques and improvised new ones. Which is not to imply that the best poems are orphic, declamatory or easy to set to music (in the last case, few are), but that a poem which cannot be spoken aloud with effect is probably not much good.

I've chosen for this anthology poems I think are particularly good for speaking aloud. Some are to be cried, some are to be whispered; their rhythms vary from colloquial staccato to jazz-infected stomps. Chosen from the past and the present, and varying in style from anonymous doggerel jokes to some of the most passionate lyrics in our literature, the examples are all, I trust, lively and will sound well. The book is designed for everyone, from six years old through to any age. It forms the new syllabus of the Poetry Society Verse Speaking examinations but is also for anyone who enjoys speaking poetry aloud.

On behalf of the Society I should like to record a particular debt of gratitude to Book Club Associates and their Chief Executive Mr. A. J. Gould-Davies for their generosity in paying the fees for copyright material included in the anthology.

In putting the book together I've had help from several people, notably my colleagues at the Poetry Society, Marjorie Barton, Michael Mackenzie and our Treasurer, Bob Cobbing. I would like also to express my thanks to my old friends Roland Butter and Ronald Deed-Poll for their special and valued support. Lastly, Angus Nicolson deserves a mention for helping me nearly lose the manuscript at a crucial point.

I'm glad we recovered it; I hope you like it.

KIT WRIGHT

I

Poem

a rose
arose

and risen
raised

its head
was razed

in time
and thyme

arose
instead

SEAN O'HUIGIN

Oban Girl

A girl in a window eating a melon
eating a melon and painting a picture
painting a picture and humming Hey Jude
humming Hey Jude as the light was fading

In the autumn she'll be married

EDWIN MORGAN

I

Snake Glides

Snake glides
   through grass
     over
       pebbles
         forked tongue
     working
    never
speaking
    but its
     body
       whispers
       listen

KEITH BOSLEY

Doris

There was a young lady called Doris
Who had a twin sister called Chloris,
   One brother called Maurice,
   Another called Norris
And two more called Horace and Boris.

Now Doris was quite fond of Chloris
And she didn't mind Maurice or Norris,
   But she hated Horace
   And Horace loathed Boris

And Horace, Boris, Maurice, Norris and
Chloris couldn't take Doris at any
price at all.

ROLAND BUTTER

2

Blue Wish

When the gas-fire glows
  It tingles with a
    Low
    Blue light.
    It
Dances with a slow
  Flicker of wishing:
Wish I may,
  Wish I might

Have a blue wish
  Always burning,
    Morning,
      Noon,
        Night.

ANSON MCKEE

Somebody said that it Couldn't be Done

Somebody said that it couldn't be done—
But he, with a grin, replied
He'd not be the one to say it couldn't be done—
Leastways, not 'til he'd tried.
So he buckled right in, with a trace of a grin;
By golly, he went right to it.
He tackled The Thing That Couldn't Be Done
And he couldn't do it.

ANON

He was a Rat

He was a rat, and she was a rat,
  And down in one hole they did dwell,
And both were as black as a witch's cat,
  And they loved one another well.

3

He had a tail, and she had a tail,
  Both long and curling and fine;
And each said, 'Yours is the finest tail
  In the world, excepting mine.'

He smelt the cheese, and she smelt the cheese,
  And they both pronounced it good;
And both remarked it would greatly add
  To the charms of their daily food.

So he ventured out, and she ventured out,
  And I saw them go with pain;
But what befell them I never can tell,
  For they never came back again.

ANON

Counting-out Rhyme

Silver bark of beech, and sallow
Bark of yellow birch and yellow
  Twig of willow.

Stripe of green in moosewood maple,
Colour seen in leaf of apple,
  Bark of popple.

Wood of popple pale as moonbeam,
Wood of oak for yoke and barn-beam,
  Wood of hornbeam.

Silver bark of beech, and hollow
Stem of elder, tall and yellow
  Twig of willow.

EDNA ST. VINCENT MILLAY

The Run

The run
From Piltdown to Paddington
Is done.
End of the line.

The satchels stand in the station under the clock.

The four-coupled, three-axle engine with bogey truck
Steamless sits in the shed, its wagons empty
As Pompeii.

End of the line.

REED WHITTEMORE

Song in the Wood

This way, this way, come and hear,
You that hold these pleasures dear;
Fill your ears with our sweet sound,
Whilst we melt the frozen ground.
This way come; make haste, O fair!
Let your clear eyes gild the air;
Come and bless us with your sight;
This way, this way, seek delight!

JOHN FLETCHER

5

2

The Pasture

I'm going out to clean the pasture spring;
I'll only stop to rake the leaves away
(And wait to watch the water clear, I may):
I shan't be gone long.—You come too.

I'm going out to fetch the little calf
That's standing by the mother. It's so young
It totters when she licks it with her tongue.
I shan't be gone long.—You come too.

ROBERT FROST

The Flower-fed Buffaloes

The flower-fed buffaloes of the spring
In the days of long ago,
Ranged where the locomotives sing
And the prairie flowers lie low:—
The tossing, blooming, perfumed grass
Is swept away by the wheat,
Wheels and wheels and wheels spin by
In the spring that still is sweet.
But the flower-fed buffaloes of the spring
Left us, long ago.
They gore no more, they bellow no more,
They trundle around the hills no more:—
With the Blackfeet, lying low,
With the Pawness, lying low,
Lying low.

VACHEL LINDSAY

Cynddylan on a Tractor

Ah, you should see Cynddylan on a tractor.
Gone the old look that yoked him to the soil;
He's a new man now, part of the machine,
His nerves of metal and his blood oil.
The clutch curses, but the gears obey
His least bidding, and lo, he's away
Out of the farmyard, scattering hens.
Riding to work now as a great man should,
He is the knight at arms breaking the fields'
Mirror of silence, emptying the wood
Of foxes and squirrels and bright jays.
The sun comes over the tall trees
Kindling all the hedges, but not for him
Who runs his engine on a different fuel.
And all the birds are singing, bills wide in vain,
As Cynddylan passes proudly up the lane.

R. S. THOMAS

Who?

Who saw the smooth snow falling
All night long?
Who heard the white owl calling
Her strange, sad song?

Nobody.
Not anyone.
Not anyone at all.

Who heard the bleak wind howling
Over wild seas?
Who saw the starved fox prowling
Through ghostly trees?

Nobody.
Not anyone.
Not anyone at all.

7

Nobody saw winter walking,
Nobody heard winter talking.

Nobody.
Not anyone at all.

LEONARD CLARK

The Lady and the Gypsy

I handed her my silver
And gullibility,
And tremulously asked her
Who would marry me,
For I was getting older,
Approaching twenty-three—
At least that's what I told her:
All girls, I'm sure, agree
It's sometimes right to suffer
Lapse of memory.

She told me to be patient,
But not for very long,
For down the summer pavement
As lilting as a song
Mr. Right would wander,
Eager, gallant, strong;
And sure enough last summer
My man did come along:
If he is Mr. Right, then
Give me Mr. Wrong.

VERNON SCANNELL

Monsieur Sévère in a Black Hat

M. Sévère in a black hat
is holding little Pierre
by the lobe of his left ear.

Little Pierre is standing on tippy-toes
to relieve the pain which M. Sévère
is undoubtedly causing.

But, M. Sévère is—at heart—
a good man. He is teaching
little Pierre his French
verbs.

Poor M. Sévère is unaware
that our friend is in some
pain.

M. Sévère is unaware of little Pierre.
Little Pierre is unaware of M. Sévère.

It will take more than tippy-toes
to relieve the pain that one
is undoubtedly causing
to the other.

PETE MORGAN

Chanson Innocente II

hist   whist
little ghostthings
tip-toe
twinkle-toe

little twitchy
witches and tingling
goblins
hob-a-nob   hob-a-nob

little hoppy happy
toad in tweeds
tweéds
little itchy mousies

9

with scuttling
eyes rustle and run and
hidehidehide
whisk

whisk look out for the old woman
with the wart on her nose
what she'll do to yer
nobody knows

for she knows the devil ooch
the devil ouch
the devil
ach the great

green
dancing
devil
devil

devil
devil

wheeEEE

e. e. cummings

A Piper

A piper in the streets today
Set up and tuned and started to play
And away, away, away on the tide
Of his music he started. On every side
Doors and windows were opened wide,
And men left down their work and came,
And women with petticoats coloured like flame,
And little bare feet that were blue with cold
Went dancing back to the age of gold,
And all the world went gay, went gay
For half an hour in the street today.

SEAMUS O' SULLIVAN

Slow Guitar
(from *Didn't He Ramble*)

Bring me now where the warm wind
blows, where the grasses
sigh, where the sweet
tongued blossom flowers

where the showers
fan soft like a fisherman's
net through the sweet-
ened air

Bring me now where the workers
rest, where the cotton drifts,
where the rivers are
and the minstrel sits

on the logwood stump
with the dreams of his slow guitar.

EDWARD BRATHWAITE

Skipping Rhyme

Pain of the leaf, one two—
Word of the stone, three, four—
Foot of the dark, pit of the hand,
Heart of the cloud, five, six, and
Out!
  Skip.
Nora she had white eyes,
Mary she had black—
Helen looked in Grey Man's Wood and
Never came
Back!
  Jump.

Nora draws a green thread,
Mary spins it blue—
But Helen will not bind it till her
True Love makes it
True!
   Quick!
One, two, leaf of the pain,
Three, four, stone of the word,
Five, six, dark of the foot, hand of the pit,
Cloud of the heart, and
OUT!

ALAN BROWNJOH

from *The Swallow*

Pretty swallow, once again
Come and pass me in the rain.
Pretty swallow, why so shy?
Pass again my window by.

Pretty little swallow, fly
Village doors and windows by,
Whisking o'er the garden pales
Where the blackbird finds the snails;

On yon low-thatched cottage stop,
In the sooty chimney pop,
Where thy wife and family
Every evening wait for thee.

JOHN CLARI

Stopping by Woods on a Snowy Evening

Whose woods these are I think I know.
His house is in the village though;
He will not see me stopping here
To watch his woods fill up with snow.

My little horse must think it queer
To stop without a farmhouse near
Between the woods and frozen lake
The darkest evening of the year.

He gives his harness bells a shake
To ask if there is some mistake.
The only other sound's the sweep
Of easy wind and downy flake.

The woods are lovely, dark and deep.
But I have promises to keep,
And miles to go before I sleep,
And miles to go before I sleep.

ROBERT FROST

You Many Big Ships with your Billowing Sails

You many big ships with your billowing sails
    gliding out on the seas of the morning
with bright flags flying and the sailors crying
and the wild winds blowing and the wild seas flowing
    and above you the Bird of Dawning:

To France and Spain and the Spanish Main
    and the Isles of Australia turning
your golden bows as the gale allows
when the green wave slides along your sides
    and you lean as though you were yearning

For some far shore where there's no more
    cloud or sorrow or weeping:
you flaunt your great sails through the storms and the gales
and in the calm night ride on the bright
    stars as though you were sleeping:

Ships proud and splendid, it is never ended
   your voyage into the morning.
Though in storms and rains and wild hurricanes
you welter and wallow, you will still follow
   the beautiful Bird of Dawning.

GEORGE BARKER

Sheep

When I was once in Baltimore,
   A man came up to me and cried,
'Come, I have eighteen hundred sheep,
   And we sail on Tuesday's tide.

'If you will sail with me, young man,
   I'll pay you fifty shillings down;
These eighteen hundred sheep I take
   From Baltimore to Glasgow town.'

He paid me fifty shillings down,
   I sailed with eighteen hundred sheep;
We soon had cleared the harbour's mouth,
   We soon were in the salt sea deep.

The first night we were out at sea
   Those sheep were quiet in their mind;
The second night they cried with fear—
   They smelt no pastures in the wind.

They sniffed, poor things, for their green fields,
   They cried so loud I could not sleep:
For fifty thousand shillings down
   I would not sail again with sheep.

W. H. DAVIES

The Door

Go and open the door.
  Maybe outside there's
  a tree, or a wood,
  a garden,
  or a magic city.

Go and open the door.
  Maybe a dog's rummaging.
  Maybe you'll see a face,
or an eye,
or the picture
                of a picture.

Go and open the door.
  If there's a fog
  it will clear.

Go and open the door.
  Even if there's only
  the darkness ticking,
  even if there's only
  the hollow wind,
  even if
        nothing
                is there,
go and open the door.

At least
there'll be
a draught.

MIROSLAV HOLUB *trans.* IAN MILNER
                and GEORGE THEINER

The Key of the Kingdom

This is the Key of the Kingdom:
In that Kingdom there is a city;
In that city is a town;
In that town there is a street;
In that street there winds a lane;
In that lane there is a yard;
In that yard there is a house;
In that house there waits a room;
In that room an empty bed;
And on that bed a basket—
A basket of sweet flowers:
 Of flowers, of flowers;
 A basket of sweet flowers.

Flowers in a basket;
Basket on the bed;
Bed in the chamber;
Chamber in the house;
House in the weedy yard;
Yard in the winding lane;
Lane in the broad street;
Street in the high town;
Town in the city;
City in the Kingdom—
This is the Key of the Kingdom,
 Of the Kingdom this is the Key.

ANON

Windy Nights

Whenever the moon and stars are set,
 Whenever the wind is high,
All night long in the dark and wet,
 A man goes riding by.
Late in the night when the fires are out,
Why does he gallop and gallop about?

Whenever the trees are crying aloud,
  And ships are tossed at sea,
By, on the highway, low and loud,
  By at the gallop goes he.
By at the gallop he goes, and then
By he comes back at the gallop again.

ROBERT LOUIS STEVENSON

Lyric

A wind sways the pines,
    And below
Not a breath of wild air:
All still as the mosses that glow
On the flooring and over the lines
  Of the roots here and there.
The pine-tree drops its dead:
They are quiet as under the sea.
  Overhead, overhead,
  Rushes life in a race,
  As the clouds the clouds chase:
    And we go,
And we drop like the fruits of the tree,
    Even we,
    Even so.

GEORGE MEREDITH

I saw a Jolly Hunter

I saw a jolly hunter
  With a jolly gun
Walking in the country
  In the jolly sun.

In the jolly meadow
  Sat a jolly hare.
Saw the jolly hunter.
  Took jolly care.

17

Hunter jolly eager—
   Sight of jolly prey.
Forgot gun pointing
   Wrong jolly way.

Jolly hunter jolly head
   Over heels gone.
Jolly old safety-catch
   Not jolly on.

Bang went the jolly gun.
   Hunter jolly dead.
Jolly hare got clean away.
   Jolly good, I said.

R.I.J.P.

CHARLES CAUSLEY

Intelligence Test

'What do you use your eyes for?'
The white-coated man enquired.
'I use my eyes for looking,'
Said Toby, '—unless I'm tired.'

'I see. And then you close them,'
Observed the white-coated man.
'Well done. A very good answer.
Let's try another one.

'What is your nose designed for?
What use is the thing to you?'
'I use my nose for smelling,'
Said Toby, 'don't you too?'

'I do indeed,' said the expert,
'That's what the thing is for.
Now I've another question to ask you,
Then there won't be any more.

'What are your ears intended for?
Those things at each side of your head?
Come on—don't be shy—I'm sure you can say.'
'For washing behind,' Toby said.

VERNON SCANNELL

Hopi Flute Song

Hail, fathers, hail!
Chieftain of the Grey Flute, hail!
At the four world-points
Ye call, ye summon clouds:
From the four world-points upstarting
Shall the rain hither come.

Hither thunder, rain-thunder here,
Hither the rain-thunder will come;
Hither rain, moving-rain—
Onward now, over all the fields,
Moving rain.
And the wet earth, amid the corn,
Everywhere, far and near,
It will shine—water-shine.

trans. NATALIE CURTIS

Jazz Fantasia

Drum on your drums, batter on your banjoes,
sob on the long cool winding saxophones.
Go to it, O jazzmen.

Sling your knuckles on the bottoms of the happy
tin pans, let your trombones ooze, and go husha-
husha-husha with the slippery sandpaper.

Moan like an autumn wind high in the lonesome tree-
tops, moan soft like you wanted somebody terrible,
cry like a racing car slipping away from a motor
cycle cop, bang-bang! you jazzmen, bang altogether
drums, traps, banjoes, horns, tin cans—make two
people fight on the top of a stairway and scratch each
other's eyes in a clinch tumbling down the stairs.

Can the rough stuff . . . now a Mississippi steamboat
pushes up the night river with a hoo-hoo-hoo-oo . . .
and the green lanterns calling to the high soft stars
. . . a red moon rides on the humps of the low river
hills . . . go to it, O jazzmen.

CARL SANDBURG

Heatwave

Heat over all; not a lark can rise
Into the arching sun;
The moor like a lion sleeping lies—
Rough mane on burning stone.
Not a harebell shakes; the wild blue flags
Of wind are folded up.
Here on the hill the air is still
As water in a cup.

PHOEBE HESKETH

My Cats
(a witch speaks)

I like to toss him up and down
A heavy cat weighs half a crown
With a hey ho diddle my cat Brown.

I like to pinch him on the sly
When nobody is passing by
With a hey ho diddle my cat Fry.

I like to ruffle up his pride
And watch him skip and turn aside
With a hey ho diddle my cat Hyde.

Hey Brown and Fry and Hyde my cats
That sit on tombstones for your mats.

STEVIE SMITH

from *Aunts and Uncles*

When Aunty Jane
Became a Crane
She put one leg behind her head;
And even when the clock struck ten
Refused to go to bed.

When Aunty Grace
Became a plaice
She all but vanished sideways on;
Except her nose
And pointed toes
The rest of her was gone.

When Aunty Jill
Became a Pill
She stared all day through dark-blue glass;
And always sneered
When men appeared
To ask her how she was.

When Uncle Jake
Became a Snake
He never found it out;
And so as no one mentions it
One sees him still about.

MERVYN PEAKE

Early Shift on the Evening Standard News Desk

Fog Chaos Grips South

A thick blanket of fog lay across Southern England this
morning like a thick blanket—

'Don't let's call it a thick blanket today Joe, let's call it a
sodden yellow eiderdown.'

'Are you insane?'

ADRIAN MITCHELL

The Last Song of Billy the Kid

I'll tell you the story of Billy the Kid
I'll tell of the things that this young outlaw did
Way out in the West when the country was young,
When the gun was the law and the law was a gun.

Now the Mexican maidens play guítars and sing
Songs about Billy, the boy bandit-king
But with drinkin' and gamblin' he come to his end
Shot down by Pat Garrett who once was his friend.

Pat Garrett rode up to the window that night,
The desert was still and the moonlight was bright,
Pat listened outside while the Kid told his tale
Of shooting the guard in the Las Cruces jail.

'I rode down the border and robbed in Juaréz,
I drank to the ladies the happiest of days,
My picture is posted from Texas to Maine
And women and ridin' and robbin's my game.'

All the while Billy bragged Pat waited outside.
Bill said to his friends, 'I ain't satisfied.
Twenty-one men I have put bullets through,
The sherrif, Pat Garrett, must make twenty-two.'

22

Then Pat Garrett fired and his thumb-buster cracked.
Billy fell dead, he was blowed through the back.
Pat rode away, left the Kid lying dead,
And this is the last song of Billy the Kid.

ANON

Colonel Fazackerley

Colonel Fazackerley Butterworth-Toast
Bought an old castle complete with a ghost,
But someone or other forgot to declare
To Colonel Fazack that the spectre was there.

On the very first evening, while waiting to dine,
The Colonel was taking a fine sherry wine,
When the ghost, with a furious flash and a flare,
Shot out of the chimney and shivered, 'Beware!'

Colonel Fazackerley put down his glass
And said, 'My dear fellow, that's really first class!
I just can't conceive how you do it at all.
I imagine you're going to a Fancy Dress Ball?'

At this, the dread ghost gave a withering cry.
Said the Colonel (his monocle firm in his eye),
'Now just how you do it I wish I could think.
Do sit down and tell me, and please have a drink.'

The ghost in his phosphorous cloak gave a roar
And floated about between ceiling and floor.
He walked through a wall and returned through a pane
And backed up the chimney and came down again.

Said the Colonel, 'With laughter I'm feeling quite weak!'
(As trickles of merriment ran down his cheek).
'My house-warming party I hope you won't spurn.
You *must* say you'll come and you'll give us a turn!'

At this, the poor spectre—quite out of his wits—
Proceeded to shake himself almost to bits.
He rattled his chains and he clattered his bones
And he filled the whole castle with mumbles and groans.

But Colonel Fazackerley, just as before,
Was simply delighted and called out, 'Encore!'
At which the ghost vanished, his efforts in vain,
And never was seen at the castle again.

'Oh dear, what a pity!' said Colonel Fazack.
'I don't know his name, so I won't call him back.'
And then with a smile that was hard to define,
Colonel Fazackerley went in to dine.

CHARLES CAUSLEY

3

Entrance to a Lane

A man came

    tasting

silence like water
water like silence

      silence tasting like water
      water like tasting silence

and

  at the end

      well water

     well

     silence

ALASDAIR CLAYRE

In a Corner of Eden

In a corner of Eden
the one-horned black
rare rhinoceros slept in the shade
water among the reeds softly swam
yellow and green the ripening melons hang
softly slept.
In the hot light once
he went, stinking shade drops
dark over his head,
in Eden once
easy-bellied he lay
and breathed a gentle breath such as yellow
fruit or any sleeping beast may.

PETER LEVI S.J.

Like Rain it Sounded

Like Rain it sounded till it curved
And then I knew 'twas Wind—
It walked as wet as any Wave
But swept as dry as sand—
When it had pushed itself away
To some remotest Plain
A coming as of Hosts was heard
That was indeed the Rain—
It filled the Wells, it pleased the Pools
It warbled in the Road—
It pulled the spigot from the Hills
And let the Floods abroad,—
It loosened acres, lifted seas
The sites of Centres stirred
Then like Elijah rode away
Upon a Wheel of Cloud.

EMILY DICKINSON

The Lost Heifer

When the black herds of the rain were grazing
In the gap of the pure cold wind
And the watery haze of the hazel
Brought her into my mind,
I thought of the last honey by the water
That no hive can find.

Brightness was drenching through the branches
When she wandered again,
Turning the silver out of dark grasses
Where the skylark had lain,
And her voice coming softly over the meadow
Was the mist becoming rain.

AUSTIN CLARKE

Trades

I want to be a carpenter,
To work all day long in clean wood,
Shaving it into little thin slivers
Which screw up into curls behind my plane;
Pounding square, black nails into white boards,
With the claws of my hammer glistening
Like the tongue of a snake.
I want to shingle a house,
Sitting on the ridge pole in a bright breeze.
I want to put the shingles on neatly,
Taking great care that each is directly between two
    others.
I want my hands to have the tang of wood:
Spruce, Cedar, Cypress.
I want to draw a line on a board with a flat pencil,
And then saw along that line,
With the sweet-smelling sawdust piling up in a
    yellow heap at my feet.

That is the life!
Heigh-ho!
It is much easier than to write this poem.

AMY LOWELL

The Poem

It is only a little twig
With a green bud at the end;
But if you plant it,
And water it,
And set it where the sun will be above it,
It will grow into a tall bush
With many flowers,
And leaves which thrust hither and thither
Sparkling.
From its roots will come freshness,
And beneath it the grass-blades
Will bend and recover themselves,
And clash one upon another
In the blowing wind.

But if you take my twig
And throw it into a closet
With mousetraps and blunted tools,
It will shrivel and waste.
And, some day,
When you open the door,
You will think it an old twisted nail,
And sweep it into the dust bin
With other rubbish.

AMY LOWELL

Songs of Experience: Introduction

Hear the voice of the Bard!
Who Present, Past, & Future sees;
The Holy Word
Whose ears have heard
That walk'd among the ancient trees,

Calling the lapsed Soul,
And weeping in the evening dew;
That might controll
The starry pole,
And fallen, fallen light renew!

'O Earth, O Earth, return!
'Arise from out the dewy grass;
'Night is worn,
'And the morn
'Rises from the slumberous mass.

'Turn away no more;
'Why wilt thou turn away?
'The starry floor,
'The wat'ry shore,
'Is giv'n thee till the break of day.'

WILLIAM BLAKE

Encounter with a God

Ono-no-Komache the poetess
sat on the ground among her flowers,
sat in her delicate-patterned dress
thinking of the rowers,
thinking of the god Daikoku.

Thinking of the rock pool
and carp in the waterfall at night.
Daikoku in accordance with the rule
is beautiful, she said, with a slight
tendency to angles.

But Daikoku came
who had been drinking all night
with the greenish gods of chance and fame.
He was rotund standing in the moonlight,
with a round, white paunch.

29

Who said
I am not beautiful,
I do not wish to be wonderfully made,
I am not intoxicated, dutiful daughter,
and I will not be in a poem.

But the poetess sat still
holding her head and making verses:
'How intricate and peculiarly well-
arranged the symmetrical belly-purses
of Lord Daikoku.'

KEITH DOUGLAS

Lord of the Dance

I danced in the morning
When the world was begun,
And I danced in the moon
And the stars and the sun
And I came down from heaven
And I danced on the earth—
At Bethlehem I had my birth.

Dance then wherever you may be;
I am the Lord of the Dance, said he,
I'll lead you all, wherever you may be,
I will lead you all in the Dance, said he.

I danced for the scribe
And the pharisee,
But they would not dance
And they couldn't follow me;
I danced for the fishermen,
For James and John—
They came with me
And the dance went on.

I danced on the Sabbath
And I cured the lame;

The holy people
Said it was a shame;
They whipped and they stripped
And they hung me high,
And they left me there
On a Cross to die.

I danced on a Friday
When the sky turned black—
It's hard to dance
With the devil on your back;
They buried my body
And they thought I'd gone—
But I am the dance
And I still go on.

They cut me down
And I leap up high—
I am the life
That'll never, never die;
I'll live in you
If you'll live in me—
I am the Lord
Of the Dance, said he.

Dance then wherever you may be;
I am the Lord of the Dance, said he,
I'll lead you all, wherever you may be,
I will lead you all in the Dance, said he.

ANON

Fairy Tale

He built himself a house,
          his foundations,
          his stones,
          his walls,
          his roof overhead,
          his chimney and smoke,
          his view from the window.

He made himself a garden,
> his fence,
> his thyme,
> his earthworm,
> his evening dew.

He cut out his bit of sky above.

And he wrapped the garden in the sky
and the house in the garden
and packed the lot in a handkerchief

and went off
lone as an arctic fox
through the cold
unending
rain
into the world.

MIROSLAV HOLUB *trans.* IAN MILNER
and GEORGE THEINER

The Great Panjandrum

So she went into the garden
to cut a cabbage-leaf
to make an apple-pie;
and at the same time
a great she-bear, coming down the street,
pops its head into the shop.
What? no soap?
> So he died,
and she very imprudently married the Barber:
and there were present
the Picninnies,
> and the Joblillies,
> > And the Garyulies,
and the great Panjandrum himself,
with the little round button at top;
and they all fell to playing the game of catch-as-catch-can,
till the gunpowder ran out at the heels of their boots.

SAMUEL FOOTE

The Willows of Massachusetts

Animal willows of November
in pelt of gold enduring when all else
has let go all ornament
and stands naked in the cold.
Cold shine of sun on swamp water,
cold caress of slant beam on bough,
gray light on brown bark.
Willows—last to relinquish a leaf,
curious, patient, lion-headed, tense
with energy, watching
the serene cold through a curtain
of tarnished strands.

DENISE LEVERTOV

The Way through the Woods

They shut the road through the woods
Seventy years ago.
Weather and rain have undone it again
And now you would never know
There was once a road through the woods
Before they planted the trees.
It is underneath the coppice and heath
And the thin anemones.
Only the keeper sees
That, where the ring-dove broods,
And the badgers roll at ease,
There was once a road through the woods.

Yet, if you enter the woods
Of a summer evening late,
When the night-air cools on the trout-ringed pools
Where the otter whistles his mate,
(They fear not men in the woods
Because they see so few)
You will hear the beat of a horse's feet,

33

And the swish of a skirt in the dew,
Steadily cantering through
The misty solitudes,
As though they perfectly knew
The old lost road through the woods . . .
But there is no road through the woods.

RUDYARD KIPLING

from *A Runnable Stag*

When the pods went pop on the broom, green broom,
    And apples began to be golden-skinned,
We harboured a stag in the Priory coomb,
    And we feathered his trail up-wind, up-wind,
    We feathered his trail up-wind—
        A stag of warrant, a stag, a stag,
        A runnable stag, a kingly crop,
        Brow, bay and tray and three on top,
        A stag, a runnable stag . . .

For a matter of twenty miles and more,
    By the densest hedge and the highest wall,
Through herds of bullocks he baffled the lore
    Of harbourer, huntsman, hounds and all,
    Of harbourer, hounds and all—
        The stag of warrant, the wily stag,
        For twenty miles, and five and five,
        He ran, and he never was caught alive,
        This stag, this runnable stag . . .

Three hundred gentlemen, able to ride,
    Three hundred horses as gallant and free,
Beheld him escape on the evening tide,
    Far out till he sank in the Severn Sea,
    Till he sank in the depths of the sea—
        The stag, the buoyant stag, the stag
        That slept at last in a jewelled bed
        Under the sheltering ocean spread,
        The stag, the runnable stag.

JOHN DAVIDSON

34

All Day I Hear the Noise of Waters

All day I hear the noise of waters
    Making moan,
Sad as the seabird is when going
    Forth alone
He hears the winds cry to the waters'
    Monotone.

The grey winds, the cold winds are blowing
    Where I go.
I hear the noise of many waters
    Far below.
All day, all night, I hear them flowing
    To and fro.

JAMES JOYCE

The Taxis

In the first taxi he was alone tra-la,
No extras on the clock. He tipped ninepence
But the cabby, while he thanked him, looked askance
As though to suggest someone had bummed a ride.

In the second taxi he was alone tra-la
But the clock showed sixpence extra: he tipped according
And the cabby from out of his muffler said: 'Make sure
You have left nothing behind tra-la between you'.

In the third taxi he was alone tra-la
But the tip-up seats were down and there was an extra
Charge of one-and-sixpence and an odd
Scent that reminded him of a trip to Cannes.

As for the fourth taxi, he was alone
Tra-la when he hailed it but the cabby looked
Through him and said: 'I can't tra-la well take
So many people, not to speak of the dog.'

LOUIS MACNEICE

The Orange Poem

Not very long ago
One morning
I sat in my orange room
With my orange pencil
Eating an orange.

This,
I began to write,
Is the orange poem.
I shall become known
As the orange poet

For inventing
And first writing
The original
Perfect
And now famous

ORANGE POEM
Which this is.
Having written which
In my orange room
With my orange pencil

I turned over a new leaf
Which this is.
Meanwhile,
Inside the orange poem
A small man

With an orange pencil
Sat in an orange room
Eating an orange.
This, he began to write,
Is the orange poem.

GEORGE MACBETH

36

The Apple's Song

Tap me with your finger,
rub me with your sleeve,
hold me, sniff me, peel me
curling round and round
till I burst out white and cold
from my tight red coat
and tingle in your palm
as if I'd melt and breathe
a living pomander
waiting for the minute
of joy when you lift me
to your mouth and crush me
and in taste and fragrance
I race through your head
in my dizzy dissolve.

I sit in the bowl
in my cool corner
and watch you as you pass
smoothing your apron.
Are you thirsty yet?
My eyes are shining.

EDWIN MORGAN

Sixteen Dogs, Cats, Rats and Bats
(for Sophie)

Sixteen dogs and sixteen cats
Went chasing after sixteen rats.
The sixteen rats were full of fear
And wished that they were bats, in air.
No sooner wished than so they were,
The sixteen rats were sixteen bats
Safe above all dogs and cats,
And to and fro, and fro and to,
About the sky all night they flew,
Leaving the sixteen cats to howl
And the sixteen dogs to growl.

37

They did not like it in the sky
Where all their food was moth or fly,
They had no cheese, they licked no butter,
They slept behind a leaky gutter
Upside down, as all bats sleep,
And now they wished once more to creep
In rat-shape round a rubbish-heap.

No sooner wished then they were down
Dragging their tails around the town
And sixteen dogs and sixteen cats
At once appeared and ate those rats.

Moral: Better be a living bat
Than line the stomach of a cat.

GEOFFREY GRIGSON

The Huntsman

Kagwa hunted the lion,
   Through bush and forest went his spear.
One day he found the skull of a man
   And said to it, 'How did you come here?'
The skull opened its mouth and said
   'Talking brought me here.'

Kagwa hurried home;
   Went to the king's chair and spoke:
'In the forest I found a talking skull.'
   The king was silent. Then he said slowly
'Never since I was born of my mother
   Have I seen or heard of a skull which spoke.'

The king called out his guards:
   'Two of you now go with him
And find this talking skull;
   But if his tale is a lie
And the skull speaks no word,
   This Kagwa himself must die.'

They rode into the forest;
    For days and nights they found nothing.
At last they saw the skull; Kagwa
    Said to it 'How did you come here?'
The skull said nothing. Kagwa implored,
    But the skull said nothing.

The guards said 'Kneel down.'
    They killed him with sword and spear.
Then the skull opened its mouth;
    'Huntsman, how did you come here?'
And the dead man answered
    'Talking brought me here.'

EDWARD LOWBURY

Three Fishers went Sailing

Three fishers went sailing out into the West,
    Away to the West as the sun went down;
Each thought on the woman who loved him the best,
    And the children stood watching them out of the town:
For men must work, and women must weep,
And there's little to earn, and many to keep,
    Though the harbour-bar be moaning.

Three wives sat up in the lighthouse tower,
    And they trimmed the lamps as the sun went down;
And they looked at the squall, and they looked at the shower,
    And the night-rack came rolling up ragged and brown;
But men must work, and women must weep,
Though storms be sudden, and waters deep,
    And the harbour-bar be moaning.

Three corpses lay out on the shining sands,
    In the morning gleam as the tide went down,
And the women are weeping and wringing their hands,
    For those who will never come home to the town.
For men must work, and women must weep,
And the sooner it's over, the sooner to sleep,
    And good-bye to the bar and its moaning.

CHARLES KINGSLEY

The Fisherman

A simple man,
He liked the crease on the water
His cast made, but had no pity
For the broken backbone
Of water or fish.

One of his pleasures, thirsty,
Was to ask a drink
At the hot farms;
Leaving with a casual thank you,
As though they owed it him.

I could have told of the living water
That springs pure.
He would have smiled then,
Dancing his speckled fly in the shadows,
Not understanding.

R. S. THOMAS

Remote House

when i wake up
the house is silent.
only the birds make noise.
through the window i see
no one. here
no road passes.
there is no wire in the sky
and no wire in the earth.
quiet the living things lie
under the axe.

i put my water on to boil.
i cut my bread.
unquiet i press
the red push-button
of the small transistor.

40

'carribean crisis . . . washes whiter
and whiter and whiter . . . troops ready to fly out . . .
phase three . . . that's the way i love you . . .
amalgamated steel stocks are back to par. . . .'

i do not take the axe.
i do not smash the gadget to pieces.
the voice of terror
calms me; it says:
we are still alive.

the house is silent.
i do not know how to set traps
or make an axe out of flint,
when the last blade
has rusted.

HANS MAGNUS ENZENSBERGER
trans. MICHAEL HAMBURGER

MacPherson's Farewell

Farewell, ye dungeons dark and strong,
  The wretch's destiny!
Macpherson's time will not be long
  On yonder gallows-tree.

Sae rantingly, sae wantonly,
  Sae dauntingly gaed he;
He played a spring, and danced it round,
  Below the gallows-tree.

Oh, what is death but parting breath?
  On mony a bloody plain
I've dared his face, and in this place
  I scorn him yet again!

Untie these bands from off my hands,
  And bring to me my sword!
And there's no a man in all Scotland
  But I'll brave him at a word.

I've lived a life of sturt and strife;
  I die by treachery:
It burns my heart I must depart
  And not avengèd be.

Now farewell light—thou sunshine bright
  And all beneath the sky!
May coward shame disdain his name,
  The wretch that dares not die.

ROBERT BURNS

Carol

There was a boy bedded in bracken,
Like to a sleeping snake all curled he lay;
On his thin navel turned this spinning sphere,
Each feeble finger fetched seven suns away.
He was not dropped in good-for-lambing weather,
He took no suck when shook buds sing together,
But he is come in cold-as-workhouse weather,
    Poor as a Salford child.

JOHN SHORT

Glaucopis

John Fane Dingle
  By Rumney Brook
Shot a crop-eared owl
  For pigeon mistook:

Caught by the lax wing.
  —She, as she dies,
Thrills his warm soul through
  With her deep eyes.

42

Corpse eyes are eerie:
   Tiger-eyes fierce.
John Fane Dingle found
   Owl-eyes worse.

Owl-eyes on night-clouds,
   Constant as fate,
Owl-eyes in baby's face:
   On dish and plate:

Owl-eyes, without sound.
   —Pale of hue.
John died, of no complaint,
   With owl-eyes too.

RICHARD HUGHES

Barn Owl

Round owl,
round and white
with moonglass eyes—
a cry of fright in the wood
where movement dies.
Then windless, milky flight
in search of blood.

Stone owl,
still as stone
struck from Minerva's shield
in hayloft hole,
watching through daylight-shuttered eyes
till darkness fold
in sleep the unsleeping field.

Round owl ringed in a world alone.

PHOEBE HESKETH

43

Quickstep

Way down Geneva,
All along Vine,
Deeper than the snowdrift
Love's eyes shine:

Mary Lou's walking
In the winter time.

She's got

Red boots on, she's got
Red boots on,
Kicking up the winter
Till the winter's gone.

So

Go by Ontario,
Look down Main,
If you can't Mary Lou
Come back again:

Sweet light burning
In winter's flame.

She's got

Snow in her eyes, got
A tingle in her toes
And new red boots on
Wherever she goes.

So

All around Lake Street,
Up by St. Paul,
Quicker than the white wind
Love takes all:

Mary Lou's walking
In the big snow fall.

She's got

Red boots on, she's got
Red boots on,
Kicking up the winter
Till the winter's gone.

ANSON MCKEE

The Ruins of Lo-Yang

I climb to the ridge of Pei Mang Hills
And look down on the city of Lo-yang.
In Lo-yang how still it is!
Palaces and houses all burnt to ashes.
Walls and fences all broken and gaping,
Thorns and brambles shooting up to the sky.
I do not see the old old-men:
I see only the new young-men.
I turn aside, for the straight road is lost:
The fields are overgrown and will never be ploughed again
I have been away such a long time
That I do not know which path is which.
How sad and ugly the empty moors are!
A thousand miles without the smoke of a chimney.
I think of our life together all those years:
　　　My heart is tied with sorrow and I cannot speak.

TS'AO CHIH *trans.* ARTHUR WALEY

Montana Born

I saw her through wavering candlelight,
My sister in her cradle, one hour old;
Outside, the snow was drifting through the night,
But she lay warm, oblivious to the cold.

45

Her eyes were closed, the half-moist wisps of hair,
A honey harvest on her wrinkled head,
The smile upon her face as if she was elsewhere,
But knew the land she had inherited.

My mother there at peace, her labour done,
Their greyness gone, her cheeks were coralline,
She welcomed me, her wondering first-born son
And placed my sister's new-nailed hand in mine.

I looked through the freezing window pane,
The whitening acre bare and stretching far
That nine months hence would heave with swelling grain,
And over every distant peak a star.

And she, my winter sister, does she know
That all this homely countryside is hers,
Where once were warring Sioux and buffalo,
And covered waggons full of travellers?

But I will tell her all the Indian tales,
And show her grass-high fields, and sugar beet,
We'll ride all day along the western trails,
Missouri River glinting at our feet.

Montana born, she'll sleep beneath these beams,
And learn the simple ways, and say her prayers,
And even now she may see in her dreams
Another boy come climbing up the stairs.

LEONARD CLARK

4

Living

The fire in leaf and grass
so green it seems
each summer the last summer.

The wind blowing, the leaves
shivering in the sun,
each day the last day.

A red salamander
so cold and so
easy to catch, dreamily

moves his delicate feet
and long tail. I hold
my hand open for him to go.

Each minute the last minute.

DENISE LEVERTOV

Footnotes on Happiness

Happiness filters
Out through a crack in the door, through the net's reticulations.
But also in.

The old cat Patience
Watching the hole with folded paws and quiet tail
Can seldom catch it.

Time tables fail.
It rarely stands at a certain moment a certain day
At a certain bus-stop.

You cannot say
It will keep an appointment, or pass the same street corner twice.
Nor say it won't.

Lavender, ice,
Camphor, glass cases, vacuum chambers hermetically sealed,
Won't keep it fresh.

It will not yield
Except to the light, the careless, the accidental hand,
And easily bruises.

It is brittle as sand.
It is more and less than you hoped to find. It has never quite
Your own ideas.

It shows no spite
Or favour in choosing its host. It is, like God,
Casual, odd.

A. S. J. TESSIMOND

My Stiff-spread Arms

My stiff-spread arms
Break into sudden gesture;
My feet seize upon the rhythm;
My hands drag it upwards:
Thus I create the dance.

I drink of the red bowl of the sunlight,
I swim through seas of rain.
I dig my toes into earth,
I taste the smack of the wind.
I am myself:
I live.

The temples of the gods are forgotten or in ruins.
Professors are still arguing about the past and the future.
I am sick of reading marginal notes on life,
I am weary of following false banners.
I desire nothing more intensely or completely than the present.
There is nothing about me you are more likely to notice
                              than my being.
Let me therefore rejoice silently,
A golden butterfly glancing against an unflecked wall.

JOHN GOULD FLETCHER

A Narrow Fellow in the Grass

A narrow Fellow in the Grass
Occasionally rides—
You may have met Him—did you not
His notice sudden is—

The Grass divides as with a Comb—
A spotted shaft is seen—
And then it closes at your feet
And opens further on—

He likes a Boggy Acre
A Floor too cool for Corn—
Yet when a Boy, and Barefoot—
I more than once at Noon
Have passed, I thought, a Whip lash
Unbraiding in the Sun
When stooping to secure it
It wrinkled, and was gone—

Several of Nature's People
I know, and they know me—
I feel for them a transport
Of cordiality—

But never met this Fellow
Attended, or alone
Without a tighter breathing
And Zero at the Bone—

EMILY DICKINSON

The Travelling Bear

Grass-blades push up between the cobblestones
And catch the sun on their flat sides
Shooting it back,
Gold and emerald,
Into the eyes of passers-by.

And over the cobblestones,
Square-footed and heavy,
Dances the trained bear.
The cobbles cut his feet,
And he has a ring in his nose
Which hurts him;
But still he dances,
For the keeper pricks him with a sharp stick,
Under his fur.

Now the crowd gapes and chuckles,
And boys and young women shuffle their feet in time
        to the dancing bear.
They see him wobbling
Against a dust of emerald and gold,
And they are greatly delighted.

The legs of the bear shake with fatigue,
And his back aches,
And the shining grass-blades dazzle and confuse him.
But still he dances.
Because of the little, pointed stick.

AMY LOWELL

From the Shore

A lone gray bird,
Dim-dipping, far-flying,
Alone in the shadows and grandeurs and tumults
Of night and the sea
And the stars and storms.

Out over the darkness it wavers and hovers,
Out into the gloom it swings and batters,
Out into the wind and the rain and the vast,
Out into the pit of a great black world,
Where fogs are at battle, sky-driven, sea-blown,
Love of mist and rapture of flight,
Glories of chance and hazards of death
On its eager and palpitant wings.

Out into the deep of the great dark world,
Beyond the long borders where foam and drift
Of the sundering waves are lost and gone
On the tides that plunge and rear and crumble.

                                    CARL SANDBURG

My Grandmother's Love Letters

There are no stars tonight
But those of memory.
Yet how much room for memory there is
In the loose girdle of soft rain.

There is even room enough
For the letters of my mother's mother,
Elizabeth,
That have been pressed so long
Into a corner of the roof
That they are brown and soft
And liable to melt as snow.

Over the greatness of such space
Steps must be gentle.
It is all hung by an invisible white hair.
It trembles as birch limbs webbing the air.

And I ask myself:

'Are your fingers long enough to play
Old keys that are but echoes:
Is the silence strong enough

To carry back the music to its source
And back to you again
As though to her?'

Yet I would lead my grandmother by the hand
Through much of what she would not understand;
And so I stumble. And the rain continues on the roof
With such a sound of gently pitying laughter.

HART CRANE

Moss-Gathering

To loosen with all ten fingers held wide and limber
And lift up a patch, dark-green, the kind for lining cemetery
     baskets,
Thick and cushiony, like an old-fashioned door-mat,
The crumbling small hollow sticks on the underside mixed
     with roots,
And wintergreen berries and leaves still stuck to the top,—
That was moss-gathering.
But something always went out of me when I dug loose those
     carpets
Of green, or plunged to my elbows in the spongy yellowish
     moss of the marshes:
And afterwards I always felt mean, jogging back over the
     logging road,
As if I had broken the natural order of things in that
     swampland;
Disturbed some rhythm, old and of vast importance,
By pulling off flesh from the living planet;
As if I had committed, against the whole scheme of life,
     a desecration.

THEODORE ROETHKE

Why He Stroked the Cats

He stroked the cats on account of a specific cause:
Namely, when he entered the house he felt
That the floor might split and the four walls suddenly melt
In strict accord with certain magic laws

52

That it seemed the carving over the front door meant,
Laws violated when men like himself stepped in,
But he had nothing to lose and nothing to win
   So in he always stepped.

                    Before him went
Always his shadow, the sun was at his back,
The ceilings were high and the passageway was so black
That he welcomed the great cats who advanced to meet him,
The two of them arching their soft high backs to greet him;

He would kneel and scratch them softly under the jaws,
All that is mentioned above being the cause.

MERRILL MOORE

Cats

   Cats, no less liquid than their shadows,
      Offer no angles to the wind.
   They slip, diminished, neat, through loopholes
      Less than themselves; will not be pinned

   To rules or routes for journeys; counter
      Attack with non-resistance; twist
   Enticing through the curving fingers
      And leave an angered, empty fist.

   They wait, obsequious as darkness—
      Quick to retire, quick to return;
   Admit no aim or ethics, flatter
      With reservations, will not learn

   To answer to their names; are seldom
      Truly owned till shot or skinned.
   Cats, no less liquid than their shadows,
      Offer no angles to the wind.

A. S. J. TESSIMOND

Leaves

When sunlight
          cradles the olive tree
love creates
          in that clarity
the fabric of light
             woodsmoke
floating
          between leaves
             weaving
shadows in
          the suns silk
slowly falling
          the angle
indelible
          breaks
          the ground
perfect in its timing
          we rake stones
we rake leaves
          but let the fire go out
rake ashes
          over dry stones

STUART MONTGOMERY

The Party

They served tea in the sandpile, together with
Mudpies baked on the sidewalk.
After tea
The youngest said that he had had a good dinner,
The oldest dressed for a dance,
And they sallied forth together with watering pots
To moisten a rusted fire truck on account of it
Might rain.

I watched them from my study,
Thought of my part in these contributions to gaiety,
And resolved that the least acknowledgement I could make
Would be to join them;

so we
All took our watering pots (now filled with pies)
And poured tea on our dog. Then I kissed the children
And told them that when they grew up we would have
Real tea parties.
'That did be fun!' the oldest shouted, and ate pies
With wild surmise.

REED WHITTEMORE

Song of the Child

the child ran to the mountain
and he pulled the rocks about
—I'll take you to the cleaners you old mountain
for I'll let the fountain out

the child ran to his daddy
and he pulled his beard about
—I'll knock you off your rocky chair old daddy
for I'm what you're about

the child ran to the holies
and he pulled their spires about
—I'll strip your lead for soldiers you old holies
for your games are all played out

the child ran to the soldiers
and he pulled their guns about
—I'll teach you to play war games you old soldiers
for it's turn and turn about

the child ran to the heavens
and he pulled the stars about
—I'll have you for my bathmat you old heavens
for I've drawn the plug right out

the child ran the waters
and he pulled the dead about
—I'll wear you when you're broken you old waters
for now I'm coming out

EDWIN MORGAN

A Boy's Head

In it there is a space-ship
and a project
for doing away with piano lessons.

And there is
Noah's ark,
which shall be first.

And there is
an entirely new bird
an entirely new hare,
an entirely new bumble-bee.

There is a river
that flows upwards.

There is a multiplication table.

There is anti-matter.

And it just cannot be trimmed.

I believe
that only what cannot be trimmed
is a head.

There is much promise
in the circumstance
that so many people have heads.

MIROSLAV HOLUB *trans.* IAN MILNER
and GEORGE THEINER

My Enemies Have Sweet Voices

I was in a bar called Paradise
the fiddler from the band
                    asked me, 'Why do you stand
here crying?'

I answered him: 'Musician,
this may come as a surprise—
I was trying to split the difference
when it split before my eyes.'

My enemies have sweet voices
their tones are soft and kind
when I hear my heart rejoices
and I do not seem to mind

I was playing brag in Bedlam
the doctor wouldn't deal
              asking, 'Why does he kneel
down weeping?'
              I answered him, 'Physician,
I think you would have cried—
I was falling back on failure
when the failure stepped aside.'

My enemies have sweet voices
their tones are soft and kind
when I hear my heart rejoices
and I do not seem to mind

I was blind side to the gutter
when Merlin happened by
              asking, 'Why do you lie
there bleeding?
              I answered him, 'Magician,
as a matter of a fact
I was jumping to conclusions
when one of them jumped back.'

My enemies have sweet voices
their tones are soft and kind
when I hear my heart rejoices
and I do not seem to mind.

PETE MORGAN

Alternative Endings to an Unwritten Ballad

I stole through the dungeons, while everyone slept,
    Till I came to the cage where the Monster was kept.
There, locked in the arms of a Giant Baboon,
    Rigid and smiling, lay . . . MRS RAVOON!

I climbed the clock tower in the first morning sun
    And 'twas midday at least 'ere my journey was done;
But the clock never sounded the last stroke of noon,
    For there, from the clapper, swung MRS RAVOON!

I hauled in the line, and I took my first look
    At the half-eaten horror that hung from the hook.
I had dragged from the depths of the limpid lagoon
    The luminous body of MRS RAVOON.

I fled in the storm, the lightning and thunder,
    And there, as a flash split the darkness asunder,
Chewing a rat's-tail and mumbling a rune,
    Mad in the moat squatted MRS RAVOON!

I stood by the waters so green and so thick,
    And I stirred at the scum with my old, withered stick;
When there rose through the ooze, like a monstrous balloon,
    The bloated cadaver of MRS RAVOON.

Facing the fens, I looked back from the shore
    Where all had been empty a moment before;
And there by the light of the Lincolnshire moon,
    Immense on the marshes, stood . . . MRS RAVOON!

PAUL DEHN

Interference

bringing you live
the final preparations
for this great mission
should be coasting
the rings of Saturn

58

two years time
cloudless sky, and
an unparalleled
world coverage
we have countdown
    ten
may not have told you
    nine
the captain's mascot
    eight
miniaturized gonk
    seven
chief navigator
    six
had twins Tuesday
    five
the Eiffel Tower for
    four
comparison, gantries
    three
aside, so the fuel
    two
huge cloud of
    one
a perfect
    a half
I don't quite
    a quarter
something has clearly
    an eighth
we do not have lift-off
    a sixteenth
we do not have lift-off
    a thirty-second
we do not have lift-off
    a sixty-fourth
we do not have lift-off
    a hundred and twenty-eighth
wo de nat hove loft-iff

EDWIN MORGAN

Limbo

And limbo stick is the silence in front of me
limbo

limbo
limbo like me
limbo
limbo like me

long dark night is the silence in front of me
limbo
limbo like me

stick hit sound
and the ship like it ready

stick hit sound
and the dark still steady

limbo
limbo like me

long dark deck and the water surrounding me
long dark deck and the silence is over me

limbo
limbo like me

stick is the whip
and the dark deck is slavery

stick is the whip
and the dark deck is slavery

limbo
limbo like me

drum stick knock
and the darkness is over me

knees spread wide
and the water is hiding me

limbo
limbo like me

knees spread wide
and the dark ground is under me

down
down
down

and the drummer is calling me

limbo
limbo like me

sun coming up
and the drummers are praising me

out of the dark
and the dumb gods are raising me

up
up
up

and the music is saving me

hot
slow
step

on the burning ground.

EDWARD BRATHWAITE

Note: Edward Brathwaite writes that the limbo dance is said
to have originated—as a necessary therapy—after the
experience of the cramped conditions between the slave-ship
decks of the Middle Passage.

from *The Old Cumberland Beggar*

          . . . She who tends
The toll-gate, when in summer at her door
She turns her wheel, if on the road she sees
The aged Beggar coming, quits her work,
And lifts the latch for him that he may pass.
The post-boy, when his rattling wheels o'ertake
The aged Beggar in the woody lane,
Shouts to him from behind; and, if thus warned
The old Man does not change his course, the boy
Turns with less noisy wheels to the roadside,
And passes gently by—without a curse
Upon his lips, or anger in his heart.
He travels on, a solitary Man;
His age has no companion. On the ground
His eyes are turned, and, as he moves along,
They move along the ground; and evermore,
Instead of common and habitual sight
Of fields with rural works, of hill and dale,
And the blue sky, one little span of earth
Is all his prospect. Thus, from day to day,
Bow-bent, his eyes for ever on the ground,
He plies his weary journey; seeing still,
And seldom knowing that he sees, some straw,
Some scattered leaf, or marks which, in one track,
The nails of cart or chariot-wheel have left
Impressed on the white road,—in the same line,
At distance still the same. Poor Traveller!
His staff trails with him; scarcely do his feet
Disturb the summer dust; he is so still
In look and motion, that the cottage curs,
Ere he have passed the door, will turn away,
Weary of barking at him. Boys and girls,
The vacant and the busy, maids and youths,
And urchins newly breeched—all pass him by;
Him even the slow-paced wagon leaves behind.

WILLIAM WORDSWORTH

The Cruel Mother

She sat down below a thorn,
  Fine flowers in the valley
And there she has her sweet babe born.
  And the green leaves they grow rarely.

'Smile na sae sweet, my bonnie babe,
An ye smile sae sweet, ye'll smile me dead.'

She's taen out her little pen-knife,
And twinn'd the sweet babe o its life.

She's howket a grave by the light o the moon,
And there she's buried her sweet babe in.

As she was going to the church,
She saw a sweet babe in the porch.

'O sweet babe, an thou were mine,
I wad cleed thee in the silk so fine.'

'O mother dear, when I was thine,'
  Fine flowers in the valley
'You did na prove to me sae kind.'
  And the green leaves they grow rarely.

ANON

Coroner's Jury

He was the doctor up to Combe,
Quiet-spoke, dark, weared a moustache,
And one night his wife's mother died
After her meal, and he was tried
          For poisoning her.

Evidence comes up dark's a bag,
But onions is like arsenic:
'Twas eating they, his lawyer said,
And rabbit, 'fore she went to bed,
          That took her off.

Jury withdrew. 'He saved my child,'
Says 'Lias Lee. 'Think to his wife,'
Says one. 'I tell 'ee, a nit's life
That there old 'ooman lead 'em both,
             Tedious old toad.'

'Give 'en six months,' says Easy Joe.
'You can't do that, sirs,' foreman said,
''Tis neck or nothing, yes or no.'
'All right then, sir,' says Joe. ''Tis no,
             Not guilty, sir.'

'You, Jabez Halls?' 'I bring it in
Rabbit and onions; that's my thought.
If that didn't kill her, sirs, it ought,
To her age.' So us brought it in
             Rabbit and onions.

Doctor went free, but missis died
Soon afterward, she broke her heart.
Still Doctor bide on twenty year
Walking the moors, keeping apart
             And quiet, like.

L. A. G. STRONG

Man Cursing the Sea

Someone
just climbed to the top of the cliff
and started cursing the sea:

Stupid water, stupid pregnant water,
slimy copy of the sky,
hesitant hoverer between the sun and the moon,
pettifogging reckoner of shells,
fluid, loud-mouthed bull,
fertilizing the rocks with his blood,
suicidal sword
splintering itself on any promontory,
hydra, fragmenting the night,

64

breathing salty clouds of silence,
spreading jelly-like wings
in vain, in vain,
gorgon, devouring its own body,

water, you absurd flat skull of water—

Thus for a while he cursed the sea,
which licked his footprints in the sand
like a wounded dog.

And then he came down
and stroked
the small immense stormy mirror of the sea.

There you are, water, he said,
and went his way.

MIROSLAV HOLUB *trans.* IAN MILNER
and GEORGE THEINER

The Seafarer

Wild were the waves when I took my turn,
The arduous night-watch, standing at the prow
While the boat tossed near the rocks. My feet
Were tortured by frost, fettered
In frozen chains; fierce anguish clutched
At my heart; passionate longings maddened
The mind of the sea-weary man. Prosperous men,
Living on land, do not begin to understand
How I, carworn and cut off from my kinsmen,
Have as an exile endured the winter
On the icy sea . . .
Icicles hung round me; hail showers flew.
The only sound there, was of the sea booming—
The ice-cold wave—and at times the song of the swan.
The cry of the gannet was all my gladness,
The call of the curlew, not the laughter of men.
The mewing gull, not the sweetness of mead.
There, storms echoed off the rocky cliffs; the icy-feathered tern

Answered them; and often the eagle,
Dewy-winged, screeched overhead. No protector
Could console the cheerless man.

ANGLO-SAXON: *trans.* KEVIN CROSSLEY-HOLLAND

Evolution

One wave
sucking the shingle
and three birds
in a white sky

one man
and one idea
two workmen
and a concrete mixer

one wave
shingle
white walls
bird and sky

two workmen
and a concrete mixer

white walls
wave and windows
bird and sky

wave and white rooms
walls and windows
lights and sky

five hundred men
and a computer

desks and days
white walls
lights and
one computer

66

rooms and windows
desks and lights
lights and days
and days and rooms

desks and rooms
days and lights
daylight in
dayrooms
and days
in desks
and days
in days

and one man
mad
dreaming of

one wave
sucking the shingle
and three birds
in a wide sky

EDWIN BROCK

Harp Song of the Dane Women

What is a Woman that you forsake her,
And the hearth-fire and the home-acre,
To go with the old grey Widow-maker?

She has no house to lay a guest in—
But one chill bed for all to rest in,
That the pale suns and the stray bergs nest in.

She has no strong white arms to fold you,
But the ten-times-fingering weed to hold you—
Out on the rocks where the tide has rolled you.

Yet, when the signs of summer thicken,
And the ice breaks, and the birch-buds quicken,
Yearly you turn from our sides, and sicken—

67

Sicken again for the shouts and the slaughters.
You steal away to the lapping waters,
And look at your ship in her winter-quarters.

You forget our mirth, and talk at the tables,
The kine in the shed and the horse in the stables—
To pitch her sides and go over her cables.

Then you drive out where the storm-clouds swallow,
And the sound of your oar-blades, falling hollow,
Is all we have left through the months to follow.

Ah, what is Woman that you forsake her,
And the hearth-fire and the home-acre,
To go with the old grey Widow-maker?

RUDYARD KIPLIN(

Death Ballad

(I don't care)

Tyson & Jo, Tyson & Jo
became convinced it was no go
& decided to end it all
at nineteen,—on the psychiatric ward.

Trouble is, Tyson was on the locked ward,
Jo for some reason on the open
and they were forbidden to communicate
either their love or their hate.

Heroin and the cops were Tyson's bit
I don't know just what Jo's was, ah but it
was more self-destructive still.
She tried to tear a window & screen out.

United in their feel of worthlessness
& rage, they stood like sisters in their way
blocking their path. They made a list
of the lies of Society & glared: 'We don't exist.'

The charismatic quality of these charming & sensitive girls
smiled thro' their vices; all were fond of them
& wished them well.
They sneered: 'We prefer Hell.'

What will their fates be? Put their heads together,
in their present mental weather,
no power can prevent their dying. That is so.
Only, Jo & Tyson, Tyson & Jo,

take up, outside your blocked selves, some small thing
that is moving
& wants to keep on moving
& needs therefore, Tyson, Jo, your loving.

JOHN BERRYMAN

Almost a Real Person

Sometimes
I am almost a real person
On good days
They don't notice
My greenish tinge
The slant of ear and eye
Or the wings folded close
To the bladed bone.

They say
'Really, dear, you're just like one of us . . .
Not like the others! . . .' and
'Some of our best friends are Martians.'
If I try hard, I pass as one of them.

Only I want to flip
Flap my great snowy wings
That could break a man's arm.
Use these strong muscles
To unfold, unfold,

The serried ranks of golden feathers
Whispering row on row
Until their narrow room is full
Of strangeness.

MONICA FURLONG

A Christmas Hymn

*And some of the Pharisees from among
the multitude said unto him, Master, rebuke
thy disciples.*

*And he answered and said unto them, I
tell you that, if these should hold their peace,
the stones would immediately cry out.*
ST. LUKE XIX, 39–40

A stable-lamp is lighted
Whose glow shall wake the sky;
The stars shall bend their voices,
And every stone shall cry.
And every stone shall cry,
And straw like gold shall shine;
A barn shall harbor heaven,
A stall become a shrine.

This child through David's city
Shall ride in triumph by;
The palm shall strew its branches,
And every stone shall cry.
And every stone shall cry,
Though heavy, dull, and dumb,
And lie within the roadway
To pave his kingdom come.

Yet he shall be forsaken,
And yielded up to die;
The sky shall groan and darken,
And every stone shall cry.

And every stone shall cry,
For stony hearts of men:
God's blood upon the spearhead,
God's love refused again.

But now, as at the ending,
The low is lifted high;
The stars shall bend their voices,
And every stone shall cry.
And every stone shall cry,
In praises of the child
By whose descent among us
The worlds are reconciled.

RICHARD WILBUR

El Greco

Flame-like limbs, tortured green
In your merciless longing I burn,
Fire of the rootless who turn
Blindly to reach for the unseen,
To touch the hidden side
Of clouds where all the tempests meet—
Blood dropping from the heart of Crete
Across Toledo's cruel pride.

Behind that feast of agony I feel
Rigid the saints on dome and wall
Who watch a praying Empire fall,
A Muslem-broken world clenched to the wheel.
In this bruised light, this lust
Of twisted flesh that finds no rest
Byzantium is grappling with the West
To mend the broken trust.

And all the lonely flesh burns in that fire,
Hung on a tree naked of branch and leaf,
A rugged gesture of grief,
Wrenching faith from the venter of desire,

Until nails crushing the warped feet and palms,
The yellow drops of blood,
Shiver like blossom on the bitter wood
And swallows flood the stretching cross's arms.

CONSTANTINE TRYPANIS

Full Moon and Little Frieda

A cool small evening shrunk to a dog bark and the clank
of a bucket—

And you listening.
A spider's web, tense for the dew's touch.
A pail lifted, still and brimming—mirror
To tempt a first star to a tremor.

Cows are going home in the lane there, looping the
hedges with their warm wreaths of breath—
A dark river of blood, many boulders,
Balancing unspilled milk.

'Moon!' you cry suddenly, 'Moon! Moon!'

The moon has stepped back like an artist gazing amazed
at a work

That points at him amazed.

TED HUGHES

Pied Beauty

Glory be to God for dappled things—
    For skies of couple-colour as a brinded cow;
        For rose-moles all in stipple upon trout that swim;
Fresh-firecoal chestnut-falls; finches' wings;
    Landscape plotted and pierced—fold, fallow, and plough;
        And áll trádes, their gear and tackle and trim.

All things counter, original, spare, strange;
  Whatever is fickle, freckled (who knows how?)
    With swift, slow; sweet, sour; adazzle, dim;
He fathers-forth whose beauty is past change:
        Praise him.

GERARD MANLEY HOPKINS

5

Field Day

The old farmer, nearing death, asked
To be carried outside and set down
Where he could see a certain field
'And then I will cry my heart out,' he said.

It troubles me, thinking about that man;
What shape was the field of his crying
In Donegal?

I remember a small field in Down, a field
Within fields, shaped like a triangle.
I could have stood there and looked at it
All day long.

And I remember crossing the frontier between
France and Spain at a forbidden point, and seeing
A small triangular field in Spain,
And stopping

Or walking in Ireland down any rutted by-road
To where it hit the highway, there was always
At this turning-point and abuttment
A still centre, a V-shape of grass
Untouched by cornering traffic,
Where country lads larked at night.

I think I know what the shape of the field was
That made the old man weep.

W. R. RODGERS

Will You Come?

Will you come?
Will you come
Will you ride
So late
At my side?
O, will you come?

Will you come?
Will you come
If the night
Has a moon,
Full and bright?
O, will you come?

Would you come?
Would you come
If the noon
Gave light,
Not the moon?
Beautiful, would you come?

Would you have come?
Would you have come
Without scorning,
Had it been
Still morning?
Beloved, would you have come?

If you come
Haste and come.
Owls have cried;
It grows dark
To ride.
Beloved, beautiful, come.

EDWARD THOMAS

They Flee from Me

They flee from me, that sometime did me seek
  With naked foot, stalking in my chamber.
I have seen them gentle, tame, and meek,
  That now are wild, and do not remember
  That sometime they put themselves in danger
    To take bread at my hand; and now they range
    Busily seeking with a continual change.

Thanked be fortune it hath been otherwise
  Twenty times better; but once, in special,
In thin array, after a pleasant guise,
  When her loose gown from her shoulders did fall,
  And she me caught in her arms long and small,
    Therewith all sweetly did me kiss
    And softly said, 'Dear heart, how like you this?'

It was no dream; I lay broad waking:
  But all is turned, thorough my gentleness,
Into a strange fashion of forsaking;
  And I have leave to go of her goodness,
  And she also to use newfangleness.
    But since that I so kindly am served,
    I would fain know what she hath deserved.

SIR THOMAS WYATT

Air and Angels

Twice or thrice had I loved thee
Before I knew they face or name;
So in a voice, so in a shapeless flame,
Angels affect us oft, and worshiped be;
  Still when, to where thou wert, I came,
Some lovely glorious nothing I did see.
  But since my soul, whose child love is,
Takes limbs of flesh, and else could nothing do,
  More subtle than the parent is

76

Love must not be, but take a body too;
  And therefore what thou wert, and who,
    I bid love ask, and now
That it assume thy body I allow,
And fix itself in thy lip, eye, and brow.

While thus to ballast love I thought,
And so more steadily to have gone,
With wares which would sink admiration,
I saw I had love's pinnace overfraught;
  Ev'ry thy hair for love to work upon
Is much too much, some fitter must be sought;
  For, nor in nothing, nor in things
Extreme and scatt'ring bright, can love inhere.
  Then as an angel, face and wings
Of air, not pure as it, yet pure doth wear,
  So thy love may be my love's sphere.
  Just such disparity
As is 'twixt air and angels' purity,
'Twixt women's love and men's will ever be.

JOHN DONNE

To His Coy Mistress

Had we but World enough, and time,
This coyness Lady were no crime.
We would sit down, and think which way
To walk, and pass our long Love's Day.
Thou by the Indian Ganges side
Should'st Rubies find: I by the Tide
Of Humber would complain. I would
Love you ten years before the Flood:
And you should if you please refuse
Till the conversion of the Jews.
My vegetable Love should grow
Vaster than Empires, and more slow.
An hundred years should go to praise
Thine Eyes, and on thy Forehead Gaze.
Two hundred to adore each Breast:
But thirty thousand to the rest.

An Age at least to every part,
And the last Age should show your Heart.
For Lady you deserve this State;
Nor would I love at lower rate.
　　But at my back I always hear
Time's winged Chariot hurrying near:
And yonder all before us lie
Desarts of vast Eternity.
Thy Beauty shall no more be found,
Nor, in thy marble Vault, shall sound
My echoing Song: then Worms shall try
That long preserv'd Virginity:
And your quaint Honour turn to dust;
And into ashes all my Lust.
The Grave's a fine and private place,
But none I think do there embrace.
　　Now therefore, while the youthful hew
Sits on thy skin like morning dew,
And while thy willing Soul transpires
At every pore with instant Fires,
Now let us sport us while we may;
And now, like am'rous birds of prey,
Rather at once our Time devour,
Than languish in his slow-chapt pow'r.
Let us roll all our Strength, and all
Our sweetness, up into one Ball:
And tear our pleasures with rough strife,
Thorough the Iron gates of Life.
Thus, though we cannot make our Sun
Stand still, yet we will make him run.

ANDREW MARVELL

somewhere i have never travelled

somewhere i have never travelled,gladly beyond
any experience,your eyes have their silence:
in your most frail gesture are things which enclose me,
or which i cannot touch because they are too near

your slightest look easily will Enclose me
though i have closed myself as fingers,
you open always petal by petal myself as Spring opens
(touching skilfully,mysteriously)her first rose

or if your wish be to close me,i and
my life will shut very beautifully,suddenly,
as when the heart of this flower imagines
the snow carefully everywhere descending;

nothing which we are to perceive in this world equals
the power of your intense fragility:whose texture
compels me with the colour of its countries,
rendering death and forever with each breathing

(i do not know what it is about you that closes
and opens;only something in me understands
the voice of your eyes is deeper than all roses)
nobody,not even the rain,has such small hands

e.e.cummings

The Touches of Loving

I love affection
When I see a hand, in
Conversation,
Touching, in love,
Another hand, my
Feeling is
Exhilaration.

Or when I see
Touched by a hand,
Fluffed out, a cat,
Conforming quietly
To the warming
Contours of a lap, I love
Affection.

And after I see these
Touches of affection between
Two I seldom see
Or two unknown to me,
I am caught for a long while
By a scent
Of recollection.

GEOFFREY GRIGSON

Triptych

Her face	Her tongue	Her wit
so fair	so sweet	so sharp
first bent	then drew	then hit
mine eye	mine ear	my heart
Mine eye	Mine ear	My heart
to like	to learn	to love
her face	her tongue	her wit
doth lead	doth teach	doth move
Her face	Her tongue	Her wit
with beams	with sound	with art
doth blind	doth charm	doth knit
mine eye	mine ear	my heart
Mine eye	Mine ear	My heart
with life	with hope	with skill
her face	her tongue	her wit
doth feed	doth feast	doth fill
O face	O tongue	O wit
with frowns	with checks	with smart
wrong not	vex not	wound not
mine eye	mine ear	my heart
This eye	This ear	This heart
shall joy	shall yield	shall swear
her face	her tongue	her wit
to serve	to trust	to fear.

SIR ARTHUR GORGES

80

The Upriver Incident

He thanked his parents for keeping still
And left them sleeping, deaf and blind
After their heavy meal,

Then stole away where the moon was full
And the dogs gave no sound.
He thanked the dogs for keeping still

And ran along the tops of the dark hills
That heaped like the sleeping anaconda
After its heavy meal,

To the bright square in the highest coil
That was the lady's window.
She thanked her parents for keeping still

And they ran together over a further hill
Like the lady's belly so hard and round
After its heavy meal,

Till they stood at the top of the waterfall,
Its deep pool where they drowned.
Let us thank waters for not keeping still
After their heavy meal.

PAUL MULDOON

The Call

From our low seat beside the fire
   Where we have dozed and dreamed and watched the glow
  Or raked the ashes, stopping so
We scarcely saw the sun or rain
  Above, or looked much higher
Than this same quiet red or burned-out fire,
      Tonight we heard a call,
      A rattle on the window-pane,
      A voice on the sharp air,
And felt a breath stirring our hair,

A flame within us: Something swift and tall
Swept in and out and that was all.
Was it a bright or a dark angel? Who can know?
   It left no mark upon the snow,
      But suddenly it snapped the chain,
      Unbarred, flung wide the door
      Which will not shut again;
   And so we cannot sit here any more.
            We must arise and go:
      The world is cold without
      And dark and hedged about
   With mystery and enmity and doubt,
         But we must go
      Though yet we do not know
Who called, or what marks we shall leave upon the snow.

Beasts

         Beasts in their major freedom
      Slumber in peace tonight. The gull on his ledge
Dreams in the guts of himself the moon-plucked waves below,
         And the sunfish leans on a stone, slept
            By the lyric water,

         In which the spotless feet
      Of deer make dulcet splashes, and to which
The ripped mouse, safe in the owl's talon, cries
         Concordance. Here there is no such harm
            And no such darkness

         As the selfsame moon observes
      Where, warped in window-glass, it sponsors now
The werewolf's painful change. Turning his head away
         On the sweaty bolster, he tries to remember
            The mood of manhood,

         But lies at last, as always,
      Letting it happen, the fierce fur soft to his face,
Hearing with sharper ears the wind's exciting minors,
         The leaves' panic, and the degradation
            Of the heavy streams.

82

Meantime, at high windows
Far from thicket and pad-fall, suitors of excellence
Sigh and turn from their work to construe again the painful
Beauty of heaven, the lucid moon
And the risen hunter,

Making such dreams for men
As told will break their hearts as always, bringing
Monsters into the city, crows on the public statues,
Navies fed to the fish in the dark
Unbridled waters.

RICHARD WILBUR

The Howling of Wolves

Is without world.

What are they dragging up and out on their long leashes
of sound
That dissolve in the mid-air silence?

Then crying of a baby, in this forest of starving silences,
Brings the wolves running.
Tuning of a viola, in this forest delicate as an owl's ear,
Brings the wolves running—brings the steel traps
clashing and slavering,
The steel furred to keep it from cracking in the cold,
The eyes that never learn how it has come about
That they must live like this,

That they must live

Innocence crept into minerals.

The wind sweeps through and the hunched wolf shivers.
It howls you cannot say whether out of agony or joy.

The earth is under its tongue,
A dead weight of darkness, trying to see through its eyes.
The wolf is living for the earth.
But the wolf is small, it comprehends little.

83

It goes to and fro, trailing its haunches and whimpering
                                                    horribly.
It must need its fur.

The night snows stars and the earth creaks.

TED HUGHES

ana perenna

ana nina na-ana danu una dana
an-anasa nana anu anis ina una
ay mari ramya amarimi rama
enma ira mariamne ariana rana ira
anné ira marienna mirima nana mirim
si tiana ana itis an-athanah tana
hanah-ita ariande ana edna ira ati hanah
an-athanah tana si tiana ana itis
mirima nana mirim anné ira marienna
ariana rana ira enma ira mariamne
amarimi rama ay mari ramya
anu anis ina una an-anasa nana
ana danu una dana ana nina na-ana

BOB COBBING

Long-Legged Fly

That civilization may not sink,
Its great battle lost,
Quiet the dog, tether the pony
To a distant post;
Our master Caesar is in the tent
Where the maps are spread,
His eyes fixed upon nothing,
A hand under his head.
Like a long-legged fly upon the stream
His mind moves upon silence.

84

That the topless towers be burnt
And men recall that face,
Move most gently if move you must
In this lonely place.
She thinks, part woman, three parts a child,
That nobody looks; her feet
Practise a tinker shuffle
Picked up on a street.
Like a long-legged fly upon the stream
Her mind moves upon silence.

That girls at puberty may find
The first Adam in their thought,
Shut the door of the Pope's chapel,
Keep those children out.
There on that scaffolding reclines
Michael Angelo.
With no more sound than the mice make
His hand moves to and fro.
Like a long-legged fly upon the stream
His mind moves upon silence.

W. B. YEATS

The Performance

The last time I saw Donald Armstrong
He was staggering oddly off into the sun,
Going down, of the Philippine Islands.
I let my shovel fall, and put that hand
Above my eyes, and moved some way to one side
That his body might pass through the sun,

And I saw how well he was not
Standing there on his hands,
On his spindle-shanked forearms balanced,
Unbalanced, with his big feet looming and waving
In the great, untrustworthy air
He flew in each night, when it darkened.

Dust fanned in scraped puffs from the earth
Between his arms, and blood turned his face inside out,
To demonstrate its suppleness
Of veins, as he perfected his role.
Next day, he toppled his head off
On an island beach to the south,

And the enemy's two-handed sword
Did not fall from anyone's hands
At that miraculous sight,
As the head rolled over upon
Its wide-eyed face, and fell
Into the inadequate grave

He had dug for himself, under pressure.
Yet I put my flat hand to my eyebrows
Months later, to see him again
In the sun, when I learned how he died,
And imagined him, there,
Come, judged, before his small captors,

Doing all his lean tricks to amaze them—
The back somersault, the kip-up—
And at last, the stand on his hands,
Perfect, with his feet together,
His head down, evenly breathing,
As the sun poured up from the sea

And the headsman broke down
In a blaze of tears, in that light
Of the thin, long human frame
Upside down in its own strange joy,
And, if some other one had not told him,
Would have cut off the feet

Instead of the head,
And if Armstrong had not presently risen
In kingly, round-shouldered attendance,
And then knelt down in himself
Beside his hacked, glittering grave, having done
All things in this life that he could.

JAMES DICKEY

Forget About Me

Among the things the sea throws up,
let us hunt for the most purified,
violet claws of crabs,
little skulls of dead fish,
smooth syllables of wood,
small countries of mother-of-pearl;
let us look for what the sea undid
insistently, carelessly,
what it broke up and abandoned,
and left behind for us.

Petals crimped up,
cotton from the tidewash,
useless sea-jewels,
and sweet bones of birds
still in the poise of flight.

The sea washed up its tidewrack,
the air played with the sea-things;
when there was sun, it embraced them,
and time lives close to the sea,
counting and touching what exists.

I know all the algae,
the white eyes of the sand,
the tiny merchandise
of the tides in autumn,
and I walk with the gross pelican,
building its soaking nests,
sponges which worship the wind,
shelves of undersea shadow,

but nothing more moving
than the vestiges of shipwrecks—
the smooth abandoned beam
gnawed by the waves
and disdained by death.

Let us look for secret things
somewhere in the world,
on the blue shore of silence
or where the storm has passed,
rampaging like a train.
There the faint signs are left,
coins of time and water,
debris, celestial ash
and the irreplaceable rapture
of sharing in the labour
of solitude and the sand.

PABLO NERUDA *trans.* ALASTAIR REID

'There shall be no more Sea'

These rolling flowing plunging breaking everlasting weaving
waters
Moved by tumultuous invisible currents of the air
Seem liquid light, seem flaming sun-ocean pouring fire,
And the heavy streaming windbeaten waves
Consubstantial with glint and gold-dazzle flashed from glassy
crests.
On turbulence of light we float.

Why then should I not walk on water? Through water-walls
Of intangible light, mirage through mirage pass?
This body solid and visible to sense
Insubstantial as the shouting host of the changeable wind
Or fluent forms that plunge under wave, embrace passing
through embrace,
Melting merging parting for ever,
Or oreads slender as a line of shadow moving across
mountain's roseate face.

KATHLEEN RAINE

88

Dover Beach

The sea is calm to-night.
The tide is full, the moon lies fair
Upon the straits;—on the French coast the light
Gleams and is gone; the cliffs of England stand,
Glimmering and vast, out in the tranquil bay.
Come to the window, sweet is the night-air!
Only, from the long line of spray
Where the sea meets the moon-blanched land,
Listen! you hear the grating roar
Of pebbles which the waves draw back, and fling,
At their return, up the high strand,
Begin, and cease, and then again begin,
With tremulous cadence slow, and bring
The eternal note of sadness in.

Sophocles long ago
Heard it on the Ægæan, and it brought
Into his mind the turbid ebb and flow
Of human misery: we
Find also in the sound a thought,
Hearing it by this distant northern sea.

The sea of faith
Was once, too, at the full, and round earth's shore
Lay like the folds of a bright girdle furled.
But now I only hear
Its melancholy, long, withdrawing roar,
Retreating to the breath
Of the night-wind down the vast edges drear
And naked shingles of the world.

Ah, love, let us be true
To one another! for the world, which seems
To lie before us like a land of dreams,
So various, so beautiful, so new,
Hath really neither joy, nor love, nor light,
Nor certitude, nor peace, nor help for pain;
And we are here as on a darkling plain
Swept with confused alarms of struggle and flight,
Where ignorant armies clash by night.

MATTHEW ARNOLD

The Dover Bitch
A Criticism of Life

So there stood Matthew Arnold and this girl
With the cliffs of England crumbling away behind them,
And he said to her, 'Try to be true to me,
And I'll do the same for you, for things are bad
All over, etc., etc.'
Well now, I knew this girl. It's true she had read
Sophocles in a fairly good translation
And caught that bitter allusion to the sea,
But all the time he was talking she had in mind
The notion of what his whiskers would feel like
On the back of her neck. She told me later on
That after a while she got to looking out
At the lights across the channel, and really felt sad,
Thinking of all the wine and enormous beds
And blandishments in French and the perfumes.
And then she got really angry. To have been brought
All the way down from London, and then be addressed
As a sort of mournful cosmic last resort
Is really tough on a girl, and she was pretty.
Anyway, she watched him pace the room
And finger his watch-chain and seem to sweat a bit,
And then she said one or two unprintable things.
But you mustn't judge her by that. What I mean to say is,
She's really all right. I still see her once in a while
And she always treats me right. We have a drink
And I give her a good time, and perhaps it's a year
Before I see her again, but there she is,
Running to fat, but dependable as they come.
And sometimes I bring her a bottle of *Nuit d'Amour*.

ANTHONY HECHT

Rumshop Girl

Walked the burnt red roads, looping the green hills
Like red ropes around nine green tons of cane,
Thirsty hours on the road under the honey sun.
Came up to a rumshop on the bright-stone way.

Ordered hard yellow cheese, thick slices of earth-brown
        bread,
Four tall beers dewed with cool keeping.
Life was good. Kicked my boots off under the counter.
It was a joy when the big girl came
With dancing step, full of sweet eyes,
Black face full of dark shining, breasts stuffing her blouse.
It was marvellous how she leaned them on the counter
Like fat young pullets, how her thighs bounced.
She clapped down the plate with a sideways look
And poured the cold beers, cold as creeks,
She stood arms akimbo, making her dark eyes sweeteyes.
Good to be hungry and eat that cheese, that soft bread.
Good to be thirsty and drink the cold-dewed beer in a gulp.
Good to be a man and see the girl, arms akimbo, make her
        eyes sweet for me.
The gleaming sun floods the red road outside;
Smell of warmed flowers, song of corn-birds, dream in the
        air.
What joy to be alive! Far, far away is death.
Suddenly the girl laughs, I laugh also, we do not speak.

IAN MCDONALD

from *Laughter*

In Iceland, when, dragged out by the dreary flatulence of the
weather, the right minutes had elapsed, and the geyser was due,

my holidaying friend,

whose face had been calm as the ultramarine silica-lined pool
before him, though perhaps raked a little by the wind, because
when the water's surface began to break apart in circular
ripples running outwards from its centre, his lips distended
laterally, parting slightly,

now,

with the furrows which flanked his mouth in curves between
chin and nostril deepening steadily as were the concentric

ripplings in the basin, and with fern-leaf wrinkles as hammocks
for enlightening eyes, round, moist as the nipple which was
forming and fast bulging into a silky bubble where the ripples
commenced and draining the basin around,

suddenly laughed—

Lento

p   HA HA HA HA HA HA HA!   f

—in the manner of a geyser when its bubble bursts, and
showers leap up in steamy paroxysms to a sustained uproaring.
Then he flopped, and at the same time the geyser fell back
into its basin, panting, while nearby vents gurgled like
lavatories, and the scattered spray faded in the wind.

WILLIAM RADICE

Ilion, Ilion

Ilion, Ilion, dreamy Ilion, pillared Ilion, holy Ilion,
City of Ilion when wilt thou be melody born?
Blue Scamander, yellowing Simois from the heart of piny Ida
Everwhirling from the molten snows upon the mountainthrone.
Roll Scamander, ripple Simois, ever onward to a melody
Manycircled, overflowing thoro' and thoro' the flowery level
                                        of unbuilt Ilion,
City of Ilion, pillared Ilion, shadowy Ilion, holy Ilion,
   To a music merrily flowing, merrily echoing
   When wilt thou be melody born?

Manygated, heavywalléd, manytowered city of Ilion,
From the silver, lilyflowering meadowlevel
   When wilt thou be melody born?
Ripple onward, echoing Simois,
Ripple ever with a melancholy moaning,
   In the rushes to the dark blue brimméd Ocean, yellowing
                                        Simois,

To a music from the golden twanging harpwire heavily drawn.
   Manygated, heavywalléd, manytowered city of Ilion,
   To a music sadly flowing, slowly falling,
   When wilt thou be melody born?

ALFRED, LORD TENNYSON

Please!

O God, do something worldly for us!
O, load us with a very large sum of money
Now,
And in any reliable currency
Allow
Us to be surprised. Fill up our dustbin
With packages of undevalued
Yen,
Reichsmark, or the more humbly pursued
Pound.
Begin
Each day with the
Sound
Of a not small cheque.
Let
Paul Get-
-ty and Barbara Hutton take a fancy to either or both of us.
Thrus-
-t several remunerative and gay
Tempta-
-tions in our way,
Such as a
Venice palazzo with a whale-
-scale swimpool, and a
Merc,
Or two Mercs. Arrange for my
Work
To be high-
-ly app-
-lauded everywhere, and re-
-warded beyond its merits. Snap

Thy magnificent fingers, be
Not skimping with largesse,
Tax-free;
For example gold
Francs,
And from untold
Swiss rolls and credits in countless
Banks,
O God, withhold
Not
O not withhold Thy hand.
But
With such mundane meaningless things, Almighty, cover us
    thick
Ageing babes-in-the-wood, and
Cover us quick!

MICHAEL BURN

The Good Rich Man

Mr Mandragon, the Millionaire, he wouldn't have wine or
    wife,
He couldn't endure complexity; he lived the simple life.
He ordered his lunch by megaphone in manly, simple tones,
And used all his motors for canvassing voters, and twenty
    telephones;
Besides a dandy little machine,
Cunning and neat as ever was seen
With a hundred pulleys and cranks between,
Made of metal and kept quite clean,
To hoist him out of his healthful bed on every day of his life,
And wash him and brush him, and shave him and dress him
    to live the Simple Life.

Mr Mandragon was most refined and quietly, neatly dressed,
Say all the American newspapers that know refinement best;
Neat and quiet the hair and hat, and the coat quiet and neat.
A trouser worn upon either leg, while boots adorn the feet;

And not, as anyone might expect,
A Tiger Skin, all striped and flecked,
And a Peacock Hat with the tail erect,
A scarlet tunic with sunflowers decked,
That might have had a more marked effect,
And pleased the pride of a weaker man that yearned for wine
    or wife;
But fame and the flagon, for Mr Mandragon obscured the
    Simple Life.

Mr Mandragon, the Millionaire, I'm glad to say, is dead;
He enjoyed a quiet funeral in a crematorium shed,
And he lies there fluffy and soft and grey, and certainly
    quite refined,
When he might have rotted to flowers and fruit with Adam
    and all mankind,
Or be eaten by wolves athirst for blood,
Or burnt on a big tall pyre of wood,
In a towering flame, as a heathen should,
Or even sat with us here at food,
Merrily taking twopenny ale and cheese with a pocket-knife;
But these were luxuries not for him who went for the
    Simple Life.

G. K. CHESTERTON

from *A Vision of Judgment*

Saint Peter sat by the celestial gate,
    And nodded o'er his keys: when, lo! there came
A wondrous noise he had not heard of late—
    A rushing sound of wind, and stream, and flame;
In short, a roar of things extremely great,
    Which would have made aught save a saint exclaim;
But he, with first a start and then a wink,
Said, 'There's another star gone out, I think!'

But ere he could return to his repose,
    A cherub flapped his right wing o'er his eyes—
At which Saint Peter yawned, and rubbed his nose:
    'Saint porter,' said the angel, 'prithee rise!'
Waving a goodly wing, which glowed, as glows

An earthly peacock's tail, with heavenly dyes:
To which the saint replied, 'Well, what's the matter?
'Is Lucifer come back with all this clatter?'

'No,' quoth the cherub; 'George the Third is dead.'
    'And who is George the Third?' replied the apostle:
'What George? what Third?' 'The king of England,' said
    The angel. 'Well! he won't find kings to jostle
Him on his way; but does he wear his head?
    Because the last we saw here had a tustle,
And ne'er would have got into heaven's good graces,
Had he not flung his head in all our faces.

'He was, if I remember, king of France;
    That head of his, which could not keep a crown
On earth, yet ventured in my face to advance
    A claim to those of martyrs—like my own:
If I had had my sword, as I had once
    When I cut ears off, I had cut him down;
But having but my keys, and not my brand,
I only knocked his head from out his hand.

'And then he set up such a headless howl,
    That all the saints came out and took him in;
And there he sits by St. Paul, cheek by jowl;
    That fellow Paul—the parvenu! The skin
Of Saint Bartholomew, which makes his cowl
    In heaven, and upon earth redeemed his sin,
So as to make a martyr, never sped
Better than did this weak and wooden head.

'But had it come up here upon its shoulders,
    There would have been a different tale to tell:
The fellow-feeling in the saint's beholders
    Seems to have acted on them like a spell;
And so this very foolish head heaven solders
    Back on its trunk: it may be very well,
And seems the custom here to over-throw
Whatever has been wisely done below.'

GEORGE GORDON, LORD BYRON

The Most of It

He thought he kept the universe alone;
For all the voice in answer he could wake
Was but the mocking echo of his own
From some tree-hidden cliff across the lake.
Some morning from the boulder-broken beach
He would cry out on life, that what it wants
Is not its own love back in copy speech,
But counter-love, original response,
And nothing ever came of what he cried
Unless it was the embodiment that crashed
In the cliff's talus on the other side,
And then in the far distant water splashed,
But after a time allowed for it to swim,
Instead of proving human when it neared
And someone else additional to him,
As a great buck it powerfully appeared,
Pushing the crumpled water ahead,
And landing pouring like a waterfall,
And stumbled through the rocks with horny tread,
And forced the underbush—and that was all.

ROBERT FROST

The Flower

How fresh, O Lord, how sweet and clean
Are Thy returns! Even as the flowers in spring,
  To which, besides their own demean,
The late-past frosts tributes of pleasure bring.
    Grief melts away
    Like snow in May,
As if there were no such cold thing.

  Who would have thought my shriveled heart
Could have recovered greenness? It was gone
  Quite underground, as flowers depart
To see their mother-root, when they have blown;
    Where they together
    All the hard weather,
Dead to the world, keep house unknown.

These are Thy wonders, Lord of power,
Killing and quickening, bringing down to hell
    And up to heaven in an hour;
Making a chiming of a passing bell.
        We say amiss
        This or that is;
    Thy word is all, if we could spell.

    Oh, that I once past changing were,
Fast in Thy paradise, where no flower can wither!
    Many a spring I shoot up fair,
Offering at heav'n, growing and groaning
            thither;
        Nor doth my flower
        Want a spring-shower,
    My sins and I joining together.

    But while I grow in a straight line,
Still upwards bent, as if heaven were mine own,
    Thy anger comes, and I decline.
What frost to that? What pole is not the zone
        Where all things burn,
        When Thou dost turn,
    And the least frown of Thine is shown?

    And now in age I bud again;
After so many deaths I live and write;
    I once more smell the dew and rain,
And relish versing. O my only Light,
        It cannot be
        That I am he
    On whom Thy tempests fell all night.

    These are Thy wonders, Lord of love,
To make us see we are but flowers that glide;
    Which when we once can find and prove,
Thou hast a garden for us where to bide.
        Who would be more,
        Swelling through store,
    Forfeit their paradise by their pride.

GEORGE HERBERT

Bavarian Gentians

Not every man has gentians in his house
in Soft September, at slow, Sad Michaelmas.

Bavarian gentians, big and dark, only dark
darkening the day-time torch-like with the smoking
     blueness of Pluto's gloom,
ribbed and torch-like, with their blaze of darkness spread
     blue
down flattening into points, flattened under the sweep
     of white day
torch-flower of the blue-smoking darkness, Pluto's
     dark-blue daze,
black lamps from the halls of Dio, burning dark blue,
giving off darkness, blue darkness, as Demeter's pale
     lamps give off light,
lead me then, lead me the way.

Reach me a gentian, give me a torch
let me guide myself with the blue, forked torch of this flower
down the darker and darker stairs, where blue is darkened
     on blueness.
even where Persephone goes, just now, from the frosted
     September
to the sightless realm where darkness is awake upon
     the dark
and Persephone herself is but a voice
or a darkness invisible enfolded in the deeper dark
of the arms of Plutonic, and pierced with the passion of
     dense gloom,
among the splendour of torches of darkness, shedding
     darkness on the lost bride and her groom.

D. H. LAWRENCE

August

It was a slow
river that slid
wide through level
country of fen
and of soft-earth
celery fields,

99

making no sound
of water all
one afternoon
but flowing dark
as leafage swept
in a wet heap,

no wind to make
its rushes creak,
stem against stem,
or rain to fall
hissing on its
taut water-skin.

It was gallons
calm as a vat
someone has stirred
and left to work
in its own time
to clarify.

It licked itself
as quietly as
a cat its fur
and no skiff came
or wherry on
the turning curds.

And but for the
flying dabchick
that sheered from my
quietness I
might not have moved
my eyes away

from the river's
porcelain surface
something must smash,
or ever known
how near the sea
downstream would flash

for a moment
as the last sun
of August died
in a closing
gap of summer
mist, autumn mist.

TED WALKER

from *The Eve of St. Agnes*

St. Agnes' Eve—Ah, bitter chill it was!
The owl, for all his feathers, was a-cold;
The hare limp'd trembling through the frozen grass,
And silent was the flock in woolly fold:
Numb were the Beadsman's fingers, while he told
His rosary, and while his frosted breath,
Like pious incense from a censer old,
Seem'd taking flight for heaven, without a death,
Past the sweet Virgin's picture, while his prayer he saith.

His prayer he saith, this patient, holy man;
Then takes his lamp, and riseth from his knees,
And back returneth, meagre, barefoot, wan,
Along the chapel aisle by slow degrees:
The sculptur'd dead, on each side, seem to freeze,
Emprison'd in black, purgatorial rails:
Knights, ladies, praying in dumb orat'ries,
He passeth by; and his weak spirit fails
To think how they may ache in icy hoods and mails.

Northward he turneth through a little door,
And scarce three steps, ere Music's golden tongue
Flatter'd to tears this aged man and poor;
But no—already had his deathbell rung;
The joys of all his life were said and sung:
His was harsh penance on St. Agnes' Eve:
Another way he went, and soon among
Rough ashes sat he for his soul's reprieve,
And all night kept awake, for sinners' sake to grieve.

JOHN KEATS

from *Paradise Lost*

        . . . Him the Almighty Power
Hurled headlong flaming from the ethereal sky
With hideous ruin and combustion down
To bottomless perdition, there to dwell
In adamantine chains and penal fire,
Who durst defy the Omnipotent to arms.
    Nine times the space that measures day and night
To mortal men, he with his horrid crew
Lay vanquished, rolling in the fiery gulf
Confounded though immortal; but his doom
Reserved him to more wrath; for now the thought
Both of lost happiness and lasting pain
Torments him; round he throws his baleful eyes
That witnessed huge affliction and dismay
Mixed with obdurate pride and steadfast hate.
At once, as far as angels ken, he views

The dismal situation waste and wild:
A dungeon horrible, on all sides round,
As one great furnace flamed, yet from those flames
No light, but rather darkness visible
Served only to discover sights of woe,
Regions of sorrow, doleful shades, where peace
And rest can never dwell, hope never comes
That comes to all; but torture without end
Still urges, and a fiery deluge, fed
With ever-burning sulphur unconsumed.
Such place eternal justice had prepared
For those rebellious, here their prison ordained
In utter darkness, and their portion set
As far removed from God and light of Heaven
As from the centre thrice to the utmost pole.

JOHN MILTON

John Milton and my Father

Milton was not my father's favourite poet.
Shakespeare was. And you got marks for that
In the Victorian classroom with the brown
Trusses of the pointed roof and the black fat
Stove with the turtle, and always blowing through it
The smell of clothes muggy with country rain.

Milton came second. You earned marks for that.
My father, a conformist to his death,
Would have believed even at the age of ten
This value judgment to be gospel truth.
But when he spoke of Milton to us, we got
Much more than the right answer from his tone.

Seated on his high Dickensian stool
From puberty to impotence, a clerk,
(The chief clerk in the corner in his glass
Box of authority) he felt that work
And the world were a less smelly school
Where seraphim and angels knew their place.

He tasted hierarchy as Milton did
And was enchanted by it: jewelled stairs
And thrones and powers and principalities.
Each night he knelt but glanced up through his prayers
To the mountain where sat golden Almighty God
With nothing over him but empty space.

PATRICIA BEER

A Case of Murder

They should not have left him there alone,
Alone that is except for the cat.
He was only nine, not old enough
To be left alone in a basement flat,
Alone, that is, except for the cat.
A dog would have been a different thing,
A big gruff dog with slashing jaws,
But a cat with round eyes mad as gold,
Plump as a cushion with tucked-in paws—
Better have left him with a fair-sized rat!
But what they did was leave him with a cat.
He hated that cat; he watched it sit,
A buzzing machine of soft black stuff,
He sat and watched and he hated it,
Snug in its fur, hot blood in a muff,
And its mad gold stare and the way it sat
Crooning dark warmth: he loathed all that.
So he took Daddy's stick and he hit the cat.
Then quick as a sudden crack in glass
It hissed, black flash, to a hiding place
In the dust and dark beneath the couch,
And he followed the grin on his new-made face,
A wide-eyed, frightened snarl of a grin,
And he took the stick and he thrust it in,
Hard and quick in the furry dark,
The black fur squealed and he felt his skin
Prickle with sparks of dry delight.
Then the cat again came into sight,
Shot for the door that wasn't quite shut,
But the boy, quick too, slammed fast the door:
The cat, half-through, was cracked like a nut
And the soft black thud was dumped on the floor.
Then the boy was suddenly terrified
And he bit his knuckles and cried and cried;
But he had to do something with the dead
    thing there.
His eyes squeezed beads of salty prayer
But the wound of fear gaped wide and raw;
He dared not touch the thing with his hands
So he fetched a spade and shovelled it

And dumped the load of heavy fur
In the spidery cupboard under the stair
Where it's been for years, and though it died
It's grown in that cupboard and its hot low purr
Grows slowly louder year by year:
There'll not be a corner for the boy to hide
When the cupboard swells and all sides split
And the huge black cat pads out of it.

VERNON SCANNELL

Vergissmeinicht

Three weeks gone and the combatants gone,
returning over the nightmare ground
we found the place again, and found
the soldier sprawling in the sun.

The frowning barrel of his gun
overshadowing. As we came on
that day, he hit my tank with one
like the entry of a demon.

Look. Here in the gunpit spoil
the dishonoured picture of his girl
who has put: *Steffi. Vergissmeinicht*
in a copybook gothic script.

We see him almost with content
abased, and seeming to have paid
and mocked at by his own equipment
that's hard and good when he's decayed.

But she would weep to see today
how on his skin the swart flies move;
the dust upon the paper eye
and the burst stomach like a cave.

For here the lover and killer are mingled
who had one body and one heart.
And death who had the soldier singled
has done the lover mortal hurt.

KEITH DOUGLAS

from *The Passing of Arthur*

But the other swiftly strode from ridge to ridge,
Clothed with his breath, and looking, as he walked,
Larger than human on the frozen hills.
He heard the deep behind him, and a cry
Before. His own thought drove him like a goad.
Dry clashed his harness in the icy caves
And barren chasms, and all to left and right
The bare black cliff clanged round him, as he based
His feet on juts of slippery crag that rang
Sharp-smitten with the dint of armed heels—
And on a sudden, lo! the level lake,
And the long glories of the winter moon.
Then saw they how there hove a dusky barge,
Dark as a funeral scarf from stem to stern,
Beneath them; and descending they were ware
That all the decks were dense with stately forms,
Black-stoled, black-hooded, like a dream—by these
Three queens with crowns of gold: and from them rose
A cry that shivered to the tingling stars,
And, as it were one voice, an agony
Of lamentation, like a wind that shrills
All night in a waste land, where no one comes
Or hath come, since the making of the world.

ALFRED, LORD TENNYSON

The Hunchback in the Park

The hunchback in the park
A solitary mister
Propped between trees and water
From the opening of the garden lock
That lets the trees and water enter
Until the Sunday sombre bell at dark

Eating bread from a newspaper
Drinking water from the chained cup
That the children filled with gravel
In the fountain basin where I sailed my ship
Slept at night in a dog kennel
But nobody chained him up.

Like the park birds he came early
Like the water he sat down
And Mister they called Hey mister
The truant boys from the town
Running when he had heard them clearly
On out of sound

Past lake and rockery
Laughing when he shook his paper
Hunchbacked in mockery
Through the loud zoo of the willow groves
Dodging the park keeper
With his stick that picked up leaves.

And the old dog sleeper
Alone between nurses and swans
While the boys among willows
Made the tigers jump out of their eyes
To roar on the rockery stones
And the groves were blue with sailors

Made all day until bell time
A woman figure without fault
Straight as a young elm
Straight and tall from his crooked bones
That she might stand in the night
After the locks and chains

All night in the unmade park
After the railings and shrubberies
The birds the grass the trees the lake
And the wild boys innocent as strawberries
Had followed the hunchback
To his kennel in the dark.

DYLAN THOMAS

We Moved to a Farmhouse in the Yorkshire Dales and Look What Happened

Let your soul roll around these horizons,
An unchipped marble with clouds inside
Buzzing around the huge green bowl of meadows.

We sleepwalk, musically, down the tunnels of this grey rock
Which was excavated by a painstaking Jacobean drunk
Who hewed out slit-eyed bedrooms and the largest bathroom
in the world.

It all looks as easy as the pink felt pig
Which lies so sideways between the upended Czech projection
screen
And the solid leather suitcase which holds no more than a
monochrome postcard.
It all looks gigantic as our first washing machine
Which shakes the landscape, whose brand-name is Jehovah.
This morning, out of its dirty-water gut, the machine produced

A synthesis of Marx Freud Blake Dylan Us in two hundred
words,
A small creature, like a golden dog but the size of an ant
And a shower of what I thought at first were hundreds and
thousands

But which hurtled towards the outstretched window
In the direction of the ionosphere. I caught one of them.
Held it for a fifteenth of a second before it burned its way
through

The palm of my hand, between the finger bones, and up up
and away.

It was, I noted, a miniature planet
Called Grain or Groin or Groan or something like that

And I saw, in that fleck of a moment, before it joined the flock
Of other confectionary planets, all the creatures on its surface
And they were, you know, they were like we want to be.

And then the speck-size planet flared away from me

And it rolled, like a soul, around these horizons,
An unchipped marble with clouds inside,
Buzzing around this huge green bowl of meadows.

ADRIAN MITCHELL

Stripping Walls

I have been practical as paint today, wholesome as bread—
I have stripped walls. I rose early and felt clean-limbed
And steady-eyed and said 'Today I will strip those walls.'
I have not been chewing my nails and gazing through windows
And grovelling for a subject or happiness. There was the subject,
Simple and tall. And when the baker called he was civil
And looking at me with some respect he said
'I see you're stripping walls'—I could see he liked me.
And when I opened the door to the greengrocer, I glinted my
eyes
And leaned nonchalantly and poked some tomatoes and said as
an aside
'I'm stripping walls today.' 'Are you?' he asked, interested, and
I said
'Yes, just stripping those walls.' I could feel my forearms
thicken, grow
Hairy, and when the laundry arrived I met it with rolled
sleeves.
'Stripping walls?' he asked. 'Yeah,' I said, as if it were
unimportant,
'Stripping walls. You know.' He nodded and smiled as if he
knew.
And with a step like a spring before the meal I strode
Down to the pub and leaned and sipped ale and heard them
talk
How one had cleared land that morning, another chopped
wood.
When an eye caught mine I winked and flipped my head. 'I've
been
Stripping walls,' I said. 'Have you?' 'Yeah, you know, just
stripping.'
They nodded. 'Can be tricky,' one mumbled. I nodded. 'It
can be that'.

'Plaster,' another said. 'Holes,' I said. 'Workmanship,' said
                                                 another
And shook his head. 'Yeah, have a drink,' I said.
And I whistled through the afternoon, and stood once or twice
At the door-jamb, the stripper dangling from my fingers.
'Stripping?' asked passing neighbours. I nodded and they went
                                             on happy—
They were happy that I was stripping walls. It meant a lot.

When it grew dark, I went out for the freshness. 'Hey!' I called
                                                 up,
'I've been stripping walls!' 'Just fancy that!' answered the
                                            moon with
A long pale face like Hopkins. 'Hey, fellers!' he called to the
                                             stars,
'This little hairy runt has been stripping walls!' 'Bully for him,'
                                             chimed
The Pole star, remote and cool as Vergil, 'He's a good, good
                                             lad.'
I crept to the kitchen, pursued by celestial laughter.
'You've done well today,' she said. 'Shall we paint tomorrow?'
'Ah, shut up!' I said, and started hacking my nails.

BRIAN JONES

A Toccata of Galuppi's

I
Oh, Galuppi, Baldassaro, this is very hard to find!
I can hardly misconceive you; it would prove me deaf and
                                                 blind;
But although I take your meaning, 'tis with such a heavy
                                             mind!

II
Here you come with your old music, and here's all the good
                                             it brings.
What, they lived once thus at Venice where the merchants were
                                           the kings,
Where St. Marks is, where the Doges used to wed the sea
                                           with rings?

III

Ay, because the sea's the street there; and 'tis arched by . . .
                                          what you call
. . . Shylock's bridge with houses on it, where they kept the
                                          carnival:
I was never out of England—it's as though I saw it all!

IV

Did young people take their pleasure when the sea was warm
                                          in May?
Balls and masks begun at midnight, burning ever at mid-day
When they made up fresh adventures for the morrow, do you
                                          say?

V

Was a lady such a lady, cheeks so round and lips so red,—
On her neck the small face buoyant, like a bell-flower on its
                                          bed,
O'er the breast's superb abundance where a man might base
                                          his head?

VI

Well, (and it was graceful of them) they'd break talk off and
                                          afford
—She, to bite her mask's black velvet, he to finger on his
                                          sword,
While you sat and played Toccatas, stately at the clavichord?

VII

What? Those lesser thirds so plaintive, sixths diminished, sigh
                                          on sigh,
Told them something? Those suspensions, those solutions—
                                          'Must we die?'
Those commiserating sevenths—'Life might last! we can but
                                          try!'

VIII

'Were you happy?'—'Yes'—'And are you still as happy?'—
                                          'Yes. And you?'
—'Then, more kisses!'—'Did *I* stop them, when a million
                                          seemed so few?'
Hark! the dominant's persistence, till it must be answered to!

III

IX

So an octave struck the answer. Oh, they praised you, I dare
say!
'Brave Galuppi! That was music! good alike at grave and gay!
I can always leave off talking when I hear a master play!'

X

Then they left you for their pleasure: till in due time, one by
one,
Some with lives that came to nothing, some with deeds as
well undone,
Death came tacitly and took them where they never see the
sun.

XI

But when I sit down to reason, think to take my stand nor
swerve,
While I triumph o'er a secret wrung from nature's close
reserve,
In you come with your old music, till I creep thro' every nerve.

XII

Yes, you, like a ghostly cricket, creaking where a house was
burned—
'Dust and ashes, dead and done with, Venice spent what
Venice earned!
The soul, doubtless is immortal—where a soul can be discerned.

XIII

Yours for instance, you know physics, something of geology,
Mathematics are your pastime; souls shall rise in their degree;
Butterflies may dread extinction,—you'll not die, it cannot be!

XIV

As for Venice and its people, merely born to bloom and drop,
Here on earth they bore their fruitage, mirth and folly were ;
the crop
What of soul was left, I wonder, when the kissing had to stop?

XV

'Dust and ashes!' So you creak it, and I want the heart to scold.
Dear dead women, with such hair, too—what's become of all
the gold
Used to hang and brush their bosoms? I feel chilly and grown
old.

ROBERT BROWNING

I Wake and Feel the Fell of Dark

I wake and feel the fell of dark, not day.
What hours, O what black hours we have spent
This night! what sights you, heart, saw; ways you went!
And more must, in yet longer light's delay.
With witness I speak this. But where I say
Hours I mean years, mean life. And my lament
Is cries countless, cries like dead letters sent
To dearest him that lives alas! away.

I am gall, I am heartburn. God's most deep decree
Bitter would have me taste: my taste was me;
Bones built in me, flesh filled, blood brimmed the curse.
Selfyeast of spirit a dull dough sours. I see
The lost are like this, and their scourge to be
As I am mine, their sweating selves; but worse.

GERARD MANLEY HOPKINS

The Seed

I am the small million,
I am the locked fountain.

Late, late in summer's dotage
When they lie gaunt and blasted,
The hollyhock tower and the cottage
Of clover, and age has wasted
The sun—then, then at last
I jump, I glide, a waif
Victoriously lost,
Tempestuously safe.

113

I go as weak as seawater,
I lie as quiet as radium.

In the dust-high caravan, in
The cabin of a bird's claw
Or sheepback I travel, I have been
In the whale, his prophesying maw.
I have occupied both town
And parish, an air-borne spirit, a
Soldier in thistledown,
A meek inheritor.

I am dry but I shall slake you,
I am hard but I shall satisfy you.

The apple contains me and I
Contain the apple, I balance
A field on a stalk and tie
A century's voices in silence,
And all the hopes of the happy
And all the sighs of the sorry
Rest in my power to copy
And copying vary.

And remember, I lie beneath
All soils of time, fears' frost,
Remember, I stir in my death,
Most missed I am least lost,
Remember, in the gaunt garden,
In the kingdom of a broken tree,
You will find after Armageddon,
After the deluge, me.

HAL SUMMERS

Acknowledgements

The editor and publishers would like to thank the following for permission to quote copyright material: Stainer & Bell Ltd, 82 High Road, London N2 for 'Lord of the Dance' from *Faith, Hope and Charity* by Sydney Carter; Rapp & Whiting for 'The Performance' from *Poems 1957–1967* by James Dickey and for 'Evolution' from *A Cold Day At The Zoo* by Edwin Brock; James MacGibbon for 'My Cats' from *Collected Poems* (Allen Lane) by Stevie Smith; Charles Causley and Macmillan Publishers for 'I Saw A Jolly Hunter' and 'Colonel Fazackerley' from *Figgie Hobbin* by Charles Causley; Chatto & Windus for 'The Huntsman' from *Time For Sale* by Edward Lowbury; Patricia Beer for 'John Milton and my Father'; J. M. Dent for 'The Hunchback in the Park' from *Collected Poems* of Dylan Thomas; Nicholas C. Lindsay for 'The Flower Fed Buffaloes' by Vachel Lindsay; Dennis Dobson for 'Who?' from *Good Company* and 'Montana Born' from *The Broad Atlantic* by Leonard Clark; Ian MacDonald for 'Rumshop Girl'; Geoffrey Grigson and Macmillan Publishers for 'Sixteen Dogs, Cats, Rats and Bats' from *Ingestion of Ice Cream*; Geoffrey Grigson and Gollancz for 'The Touches of Loving' from *Angles and Circles*; Faber & Faber for 'You Many Big Ships With Your Billowing Sails' from *Runes and Rhymes and Tunes and Chimes* by George Barker, for 'Encounter With A God' and 'Vergissmeinicht' from *Collected Poems* by Keith Douglas, for 'The Taxis' from *The Burning Perch* by Louis MacNeice, for 'Death Ballad' from *Love and Fame* by John Berryman, for 'A Christmas Hymn' from *Advice to a Prophet* and 'Beasts' from *Poems 1943–1956* by Richard Wilbur, for 'El Greco' from *Pompeian Dog* by Constantine Trypanis, for 'Full Moon and Little Frieda' and 'The Howling of Wolves' from *Wodwo* by Ted Hughes, for 'The Upriver Incident' from *New Weather* by Paul Muldoon, and for 'Moss-Gathering' from *Collected Poems* by Theodore Roethke; M. B. Yeats, Miss Anne Yeats and Macmillan of London and Basingstoke for 'Long-Legged Fly' from *The Collected Poems of W. B. Yeats*; The Bodley Head for 'Alternative Endings to an Unwritten Ballad' from *For Love and Money* by Paul Dehn; Chatto & Windus for 'Heatwave' and 'Barn Owl' from *A Song of Sunlight* (*Chatto Poets for the Young*) by Phoebe Keth and for 'The Lady and the Gypsy' and 'Intelligence Test' from *The Apple-Raid and Other Poems* (*Chatto Poets for the Young*) by Vernon Scannell; Macmillan for 'Skipping Rhyme' from *The Lions' Mouths* by Alan Brownjohn and for 'The Orange Poem' from *The Orlando Poems* by George Macbeth; Jonathan Cape and the Estate of Pablo Neruda for 'Forget About Me' from *Extravaria*, translated by Alastair Reid; Jonathan Cape and the Estate of Robert Frost for 'The Pasture', 'Stopping by Woods on a Snowy Evening' and 'The Most of It' from *The Poetry of Robert Frost*, edited by Edward Connery Lathem; Jonathan Cape and the Executors of the James Joyce Estate for "All Day I Hear The Noise of Waters' from *Chamber Music*; The University of Minnesota Press, Minneapolis for 'The Run' and 'The Party' from *Poems, New and Selected* by Reed Whittemore, © copyright 1967; Secker & Warburg for 'Remote House' from *Poems For People Who Don't Read Poems* by Hans Magnus Enzensberger, translated by Michael Hamburger, for 'Laughter: Section 1' from *Eight Sections* by William Radice, and for 'Monsieur Sévère in a Black Hat' and

'My Enemies Have Sweet Voices' from *The Grey Mare Being The Better Steed* by Pete Morgan; Jonathan Cape for 'Early Shift on the Evening Standard News Desk' and 'We moved to a Farmhouse in the Yorkshire Dales and look what happened' from *Ride The Nightmare* by Adrian Mitchell; Oxford University Press for 'Caliban: 3' from *Islands* (© Oxford University Press 1969) and for 'Didn't he ramble: 2' from *Rights of Passage* (© Oxford University Press 1967) by Edward Brathwaite, and for 'The Dover Bitch' from *The Hard Hours* by Antony Hecht; Penguin Books Ltd for 'The Door', 'Fairy Tale', 'A Boy's Head' and 'Man Cursing the Sea' from *Miroslav Holub: Selected Poems*, trans. George Theiner and Ian Milner, © copyright Miroslav Holub 1967, translations © copyright Penguin Books Ltd 1967; Macmillan for 'The Seafarer' from *The Battle of Maldon and Other Old English Poems* by Keven Crossley-Holland; the Estate of the late A. S. J. Tessimond for 'Footnotes on Happiness' and 'Cats'; Carcanet Press Ltd for 'Oban Girl', 'The Apple's Song', 'Interference I' and 'Song of the Child' from *Glasgow to Saturn* © Edwin Morgan; Angus & Robertson (U.K.) Ltd for 'Snake Glides' from *And I Dance* by Keith Bosley; Allison & Busby for 'A Case of Murder' from *Selected Poems* by Vernon Scannell; Compton Russell for 'Entrance to a Lane' from *A Fire by the Sea* by Alasdaire Clayre; Gerald Duckworth & Co Ltd for 'The Call' from *Collected Poems* by Charlotte Mew; Methuen & Co Ltd for 'Coroner's Jury' from *The Body's Imperfections* by L. A. G. Strong; London Magazine Editions for 'Stripping Walls' from *Poems and a Family Album* by Brian Jones; Richard Hughes for 'Glaucopis'; Peter Owen Ltd, London, for four stanzas from 'Aunts and Uncles' from *A Book of Nonsense* by Mervyn Peake; A. R. Mowbray for 'Almost a Real Person' from *God's A Good Man and Other Poems* by Monica Furlong; Mrs. Alison Waley for 'The Ruins of Lo-Yang' by Ts'ao Chih, translated by Arthur Waley; Harcourt Brace Jovanovich Inc for 'Jazz Fantasia' from *Smoke and Steel* by Carl Sandburg, copyright 1920 by Harcourt Brace Jovanovich Inc, copyright 1948 by Carl Sandburg, and for 'From the Shore' from *Chicago Poems* by Carl Sandburg, copyright 1916 by Holt Rinehard and Winston Inc, copyright 1944 by Carl Sandburg; Bob Cobbing for 'ana perenna'; Rupert Hart-Davis for 'Cynddylan On a Tractor' and 'The Fisherman' from *Song at the Year's Turning* by R. S. Thomas; Hart-Davis, MacGibbon for 'chanson innocente II' and 'somewhere i have never travelled gladly beyond' from *The Complete Poems* by e. e. cummings; Liveright Publishing Corporation and Oxford University Press for 'My Grandmother's Love Letters' from *The Complete Poems and Selected Letters and Prose* by Hart Crane; New Directions Publishing Corporation and Jonathan Cape Ltd for 'The Willows of Massachusetts' and 'Living' from *The Sorrow Dance* by Denise Levertov; The Hearts and Flowers Press for 'Why He stroked the Cats' from *Fugitive Sonnets* by Merrill Moore; Mrs. John Gould Fletcher for 'My Stiff-Spread Arms' from *Irradiations* by John Gould Fletcher; Miss D. E. Collins for 'The Good Rich Man' from *Collected Poems of G. K. Chesterton*; Harper & Row for 'Counting-Out Rhyme' from *Collected Poems* by Edna St. Vincent Millay and Norma Millay Ellis, copyright 1928, 1955 by Edna St. Vincent Millay and Norma Millay Ellis; Michael Burn and Chatto & Windus for 'Please' from *Out on a Limb*. It has not been possible in all cases to trace sources. The publishers would be glad to hear from any unacknowledged copyright holders.

Index